Mexican Americans

and Education

THE MEXICAN AMERICAN EXPERIENCE

Adela de la Torre, Editor

The Mexican American Experience is a cluster of modular texts designed to provide greater flexibility in undergraduate education. Each book deals with a single topic concerning the Mexican American population. Instructors can create a semester-length course from any combination of volumes or may choose to use one or two volumes to complement other texts. For more information, please visit www.uapress.arizona.edu/textbooks/latino.htm.

Other books in the series:

Mexican Americans and Education

El saber es poder

Estela Godinez Ballón

THE UNIVERSITY OF
ARIZONA PRESS

TUCSON

The University of Arizona Press
www.uapress.arizona.edu

© 2015 The Arizona Board of Regents
All rights reserved. Published 2015

Printed in the United States of America
20 19 18 17 16 15   6 5 4 3 2 1

ISBN-13: 978-0-8165-2786-1 (paper)

Cover designed by Miriam Warren
Cover photo by Joshua M. Vargas

Library of Congress Cataloging-in-Publication Data

Ballón, Estela Godinez, author.
    Mexican Americans and education : el saber es poder / Estela Godinez Ballón.
        pages cm — (The Mexican American experience)
    Includes bibliographical references and index.
    ISBN 978-0-8165-2786-1 (pbk. : alk. paper)
    1. Mexican Americans—Education—United States.   I. Title.   II. Series: Mexican
American experience.
    LC2682.B35   2015
    371.829'68073—dc23
                                2014037293

For my daughters, Alicia and Marisela; my mom, Ramona; and the memory of my dad, Francisco Felipe.

To all first-generation college students—push forward together!

CONTENTS

ILLUSTRATIONS

Figures

Tables

Mexican Americans

and Education

Introduction

In American society, education is considered the pathway for people to attain future occupational and financial success. Ideally, a child who has done well academically in kindergarten through twelfth grade (K–12) can then attend college and, afterward, reap the benefits of a mid- to high-status career or profession. However, this is not the case for many children who enter the K–12 public school system. Public school children end up on divergent paths: some are pushed out (commonly called dropping out), some finish high school in an alternative form like a continuation school or independent study, some graduate high school and go straight to work, and some finish high school and go on to college, with a smaller number actually completing a college degree. Most Americans have faith in the idea that public schools provide equal opportunity for moving up in society but also accept that students have varied educational paths.

Mexican Americans have experienced some of those varied educational paths, including the extremes of being pushed out of high school and graduating college with graduate or professional degrees. Yet overall, Mexican Americans have not experienced the educational mobility that other racial/ethnic groups in American society have. Leaving school before graduation, barely meeting requirements for high school graduation, and not being academically prepared for college are not uncommon outcomes for Mexican American students. Therefore, their schooling experiences have been characterized by educational scholars as "school failure" and defined as *"persistently, pervasively, and disproportionately low academic achievement"* (Valencia, 2011a, p. 4; italics in original). Low achievement, in and of itself, however, does not provide the educational context for *why* it occurs nor does it reflect the desire of students and their families for education. While, in general, societal blame for low educational achievement has often been placed on Mexican American individuals, families, or cultural characteristics, this text presents research and theories that challenge those assumptions and the assumption that schools have always provided equal opportunities to all students.

This text examines past and current institutional and ideological factors that have negatively affected their public school educational experiences and opportunities. These factors have included prejudicial views of the intellectual capabilities of Mexican Americans, school segregation, curriculum tracking, inadequate resources and conditions for **English learners** (ELs), cultural and linguistic bias in testing, and the lack of academic preparation for college. Schools have often shortchanged Mexican American students along with other students of color, poor and working-class students, and those considered "average" or "below average." Thus, in opposition to the dominant myth that Mexican Americans have not experienced educational mobility because they have not valued education, this text focuses on how school norms, policies, and practices have perpetuated inequalities reinforcing social, economic, and political inequalities from the larger society. Additionally, this text presents **theoretical frameworks**, pedagogies, and educational research that attempt to understand and address unequal and detrimental educational conditions with the goal of achieving "school success." These new strands of knowledge (understandings) about schooling as well as the desire and persistence of Mexican American parents and students for a meaningful education inspired the subtitle of the book: el saber es poder (knowledge is power).

Mexican Americans have always valued education. Ask Mexican American parents what they want for their children's future, and they will most likely include education and a good job. Most Americans espouse these same goals. "Go to school so that you can have a better life," many U.S. immigrants have told their children, and Mexican immigrants and their Mexican American children and grandchildren have said the same. Mexican American parents have believed in the American dream of upward mobility and, thus, have enrolled their children in school, gotten them ready and made sure they made it to school each morning, and made sure their homework was done after school. Just like so many other parents, Mexican Americans have tried to secure the best educational opportunities for their children by switching local schools or moving to access a better program or school, consulting with other parents, and meeting with teachers and principals. When inequitable treatment or unfavorable conditions affect their children, they have also not been afraid to take a stand for them.

Mexican-Origin Population in the United States

According to the U.S. Census Bureau, there are almost 32 million Mexican-origin people in the United States, a 54 percent increase in the last decade (Ennis, Ríos-Vargas, & Albert, 2011). The Pew Hispanic Center reports that Mexican Americans make up about two-thirds of all Latinos in the United States. The live primarily in California and Texas but also have sizable populations in Arizona, Illinois, and Colorado. Mexican Americans are younger than the overall population, with a median age of twenty-five years old as compared to thirty-seven years old in the population overall. Additionally, about 36 percent are born outside the United States and about 64 percent speak only English at home or speak English very well (Motel & Patten, 2012a).

Overall, Mexican Americans have a lower socioeconomic status (SES) when compared to the overall U.S. population, meaning they have lower average education and income levels. The Pew Hispanic Center reports that among Mexican American adults age twenty-five and older about 43 percent have less than a high school diploma. The median household income for Mexican Americans is almost $39,000, which is about $10,000 less than that of the overall U.S. population. Furthermore, about 27 percent of Mexican Americans live in poverty compared to 15 percent of the overall population (Motel & Patten, 2012a). They are also more likely than the overall U.S. population to be in blue-collar (e.g., construction, production) and service occupations. Their overall low SES is a critical factor influencing academic achievement and attainment. SES affects whether a student attends preschool, the quality and conditions of schools attended, resources available to support academics, **standardized test** scores, high school graduation rates, and college attendance. Therefore, SES is an important consideration in educational outcomes.

While an overall portrait of Mexican Americans is useful to examine their position in society, it is also important to acknowledge their diversity. There are those who have recently immigrated to the United States, those who can trace their families back seven generations or more, those in between, and those who have experienced a cross-national life or family. Some are Spanish dominant whereas others have been English dominant for several generations; for others, bilingualism or Spanglish is the norm. Many U.S.-born Mexican Americans watch television shows or listen to music in Spanish, whereas others would not understand the dialogue and would not relate. While the bulk of Mexican Americans continue to reside in the Southwest, generations have grown up in the Midwest, and increasingly the South (besides Texas) and the Northeast are being called home. Whether one grows up in a predominantly Mexican American, White, Black, or racially integrated neighborhood; an urban or suburban area; a military family; a poor or middle-class family; or a biracial family, among many factors, can and does affect the diversity of experiences within the Mexican American population.

Overview of the Book

Public schools are an integral component of education in the United States. Most school-age children in the United States attend public schools. Enrollment in them has been rising since the latter part of the 1980s. Data from the National Center for Education Statistics show that almost 50 million children in the United States are enrolled in public elementary and secondary schools (Aud et al., 2012). Of these, about 8 million children in public schools are of Mexican origin. The research discussed in this text primarily focuses on these public school children.

In this text, the term *Mexican American* is primarily used, but on occasion *Mexican-origin* and *Chicana/o* are also used to refer to the same group. These terms are used to represent all persons of Mexican descent residing in the United States, regardless of birthplace. If research discussed in the text indicates important differences by birthplace, legal status, or other characteristics, it is noted in the discussion. The pan-ethnic term *Latino* is used to refer to a person of Mexican, Puerto Rican, Cuban, South or Central American, or other Spanish culture or origin, regardless of race. It is used interchangeably with *Hispanic*, almost exclusively when specific research or data presented uses that terminology. Although published data and research specific to Mexican Americans were included when available, some did not disaggregate Latino subgroups; thus, some research presented is pan-ethnic, and the terminology used in the discussion reflects this. Finally, even though Latinos can be classified as any racial group, the term *White* refers to non-Latino Whites.

The research reviewed in this text reflects the author's academic background as a sociologist with an emphasis in the sociology of education and Chicana/o studies. Moreover, much of the research in education presented has a social science orientation, and thus, a substantial amount of social science terminology is used throughout the text. The glossary at the end of the text will assist the reader in understanding these and any other discipline-specific or academic terms. Likewise, the discussion exercises and suggested readings at the end of each chapter are meant to stimulate further inquiry; dialogue with fellow students, educators, and family members; and in-depth reading. In this text, the traditional sociological orientation of focusing on problems is strong, but in conjunction with research that seeks or demonstrates actions toward solutions to problems, it finds some balance.

Throughout most of the text, I use a third-person writing style, as textbooks typically do. However, since my own story and those of my family members are a part of many of the themes and issues discussed, I depart from that here. I identify as Chicana and Mexican American and grew up in a predominantly English-speaking, working-class suburb in Southern California. Growing up, my father, who stopped going to school in the eighth grade to work, held a variety of jobs, including construction, landscaping, and barbering. Eventually, he was fortunate and persistent enough to land a city job that meant steady employment, financial stability, and health benefits for our family. At home, my mother had the monumental responsibility of running our household and nurturing and supervising seven children.

My mother spoke to me in Spanish as a child, and I responded in English. Consequently, I am English dominant and understand Spanish very well but struggle speaking it with fluency. As a child, I wasn't even aware I couldn't speak Spanish very well until I was paired in sixth grade with a Spanish-speaking little girl in order to help her—so the school thought. I understood her perfectly but felt like a sock was caught in my throat trying to speak with her. (I did improve eventually thanks to high school and college Spanish and living in a Spanish-speaking community as an adult.) I consider the academic English learned mostly in college my second dialect of English (academic English is English used in school and is discussed in chapter 3). However, verbalizing it in graduate school caused me tremendous anxiety and to feel like a masked imposter because it was different from the English used with family and friends. That sock came back to my throat, and I avoided speaking in graduate school to those that I had to speak academic English to.

All of my schooling was in public schools, including college. During the 1970s, bilingual education (discussed in chapter 3) was just beginning, but in the predominantly English-speaking community I grew up in, I was not aware of it. There was, however, curriculum tracking (discussed in chapter 2) to sort students into different learning groups. I was considered "smart" in school and placed in some of the top classes through high school but, nevertheless, not fully treated as a college-bound student despite good grades and a positive attitude toward school and academics. College was not the norm in my family or community, but for my generation and social class, finishing high school and getting a "good job" was. I made it to college and graduated, but those first years were meandering because like so many first-generation college students, I spent a lot of time trying to figure it out. Since I began college not knowing what a degree was, I learned a lot about college during those first years. As you read the text, you may see parts of your own or your family's experiences or educational issues that affected you or them in some way. You may also read about experiences and educational issues that did not directly affect you or your family but that can provide you with some new insights and voices.

Chapter 1 provides an overview of past educational conditions that have influenced the experiences and opportunities of Mexican American students. The chapter begins with the theoretical model of deficit thinking, which historically has been used to blame Mexican American students for low academic achievement and justify their unequal treatment in school. Next, segregation and Americanization programs, and the activism of Mexican Americans to combat these conditions, are discussed. Segregation and Americanization programs shaped the negative environment, resources, and curriculum that Mexican Americans were provided in schools. Equally important to this history are the ways in which Mexican American students and communities actively resisted unequal school conditions using U.S. courts and organizing at various levels. The chapter also introduces frameworks that challenge deficit theory and attempt to understand and address Mexican American school achievement by considering unequal power dynamics in society (discussed more in chapter 5). Finally, the chapter examines contemporary educational indicators that show a persisting achievement gap with White students.

Major institutional barriers to academic success, including segregation, educational testing, and curriculum tracking, are explored in chapter 2. The chapter discusses the increasing segregation of Mexican American and other Latino students, despite the end of legal segregation. Increasing segregation has numerous negative consequences for learning conditions, such as lower test scores and higher push-out rates. Educational testing, considered a standard part of school, is also discussed in the chapter with a focus on the negative impact of increased standardized and high-stakes testing on Mexican American students. Similarly, curriculum tracking, another standard part of school, is examined since Mexican American students are **overrepresented** in remedial and non–college preparatory curriculum.

Chapter 3 explores the politics and policies toward language and culture that continue to affect Mexican American students. Since a large portion of Mexican American students are linguistic minorities, the chapter focuses on policies affecting resources and supports for them and the lack of value or focus of current school policies on maintaining native languages. For English learners, the conditions under which they acquire English, such as the type of instructional program, access to properly trained teachers, and the time frame to learn English, are important for their academic success. Finally, the impact of political climate and public mood on the regard and treatment of **linguistic minority** and English learners in school is discussed.

The status of Mexican American students in higher education is examined in chapter 4. Although increasing numbers of Mexican American students attend college, a gap with their White peers remains in rates of college graduation and continuation to graduate and professional degrees. The chapter explores obstacles to college, such as a lack of precollege academic preparation, financing, and being the first in the family to attend college. Additionally, beginning higher education in a community college, as many Mexican American students do, results in many vulnerabilities when transferring to a four-year university. The chapter also discusses factors that can support Mexican American students in higher education, including strategies that students develop to navigate college and resist forces that may push them out.

Chapter 5 focuses on theoretical and pedagogical frameworks and other research that aim to improve school conditions for Mexican American students. The chapter begins with a discussion of theoretical frameworks that highlight power dynamics and the role of ideological frameworks in supporting unequal power in society. Also discussed are frameworks such as community cultural wealth and funds of knowledge, which advocate accessing and integrating the strengths of Mexican American families, communities, and culture in the school environment. These frameworks emphasize the knowledge and skills that Mexican Americans develop at home and in their communities as essential for facilitating learning at school. The chapter also discusses transformative pedagogies that promote the empowerment of students, teachers, and parents as well as the development of schools as liberatory and democratic institutions. Additionally, the chapter discusses ways in which schools can build institutional supports for Mexican American students. These include pedagogies and school practices that can empower and create an environment that supports students and their parents in school.

The sixth and concluding chapter ties the theories, pedagogies, and research discussed in chapter 5 to the educational issues discussed throughout the text. The chapter ends with policy recommendations for improving the schooling conditions of Mexican American students.

Chapter 1

Overview of Mexican Americans and Schooling

Equal opportunity in American society includes educational opportunity, which has been considered the greatest equalizing force of society. Horace Mann, a leading proponent of creating a public school system in the 1830s, proposed that students of various social class backgrounds should attend the same public schools to teach common political and moral values and to minimize social class conflict. "Common schools," as public schools were first called, were envisioned to provide equal educational opportunities to children, so that through hard work and motivation, they would later be able to compete on equal footing for occupational opportunities. Thus, regardless of whether one was born rich or poor, public schools were supposed to offer the possibility of upward mobility to all members of society. This belief was, and continues to be, an important component of the American dream.

While equal educational opportunity is a foundational ideal of the American dream, it has not always progressed as envisioned. Various social classes, genders, and racial/ethnic groups have experienced varying success with social mobility, including educational mobility. In fact, despite the radical idea he had for his day and age of establishing a publicly funded school system, Horace Mann did not include all races and ethnic groups in his vision of public schooling for children. Historically, various racial/ethnic groups—based on their perceived abilities or social status—were provided segregated schooling and differentiated curriculum or were discouraged or excluded from schooling altogether. Therefore, not all social groups have been treated equally, cutting short, modifying, or not allowing their educational mobility to begin, regardless of motivation and hard work. Educational mobility has been influenced by social, economic, and political conditions that in turn affected educational norms, structures, and policies. While these norms, structures, and policies have facilitated mobility for some people, they have created barriers for others.

Many factors of Mexican American schooling have negatively affected this group's educational achievement, and this chapter examines several of these factors in order to provide insight to their educational history. The chapter begins with an overview of a model called deficit thinking. This framework has been influential in conceptualizing Mexican Americans negatively and justifying their educational treatment. Next, major conditions that have adversely affected Mexican American schooling are discussed. This is followed by a brief introduction of theories (discussed in more detail in chapter 5) that provide alternative perspectives to the deficit thinking model. Finally, the chapter presents contemporary indicators of academic achievement (e.g., graduation rates) to understand the current educational situation of Mexican Americans in comparison to other racial/ethnic groups.

Genetic and Cultural Deficit Thinking

When examining events, it is important to consider the dominant ideologies that have shaped them. Events in society do not happen in isolation but are often shaped by ideological frameworks that guide and influence thinking and action around an issue. This has been the case with the schooling of Mexican American students. Educational conditions and policies for Mexican Americans have been influenced by a model called deficit thinking. Deficit thinking is premised on the belief that people lack certain abilities or characteristics that explain an unequal and inferior position in the various sectors of society (e.g., the labor market). In the educational arena, Valencia (1997a) states that the deficit thinking model is a theory "positing that the student who fails in school does so because of internal deficits or deficiencies. Such deficits manifest, it is alleged, in limited intellectual abilities, linguistic shortcomings, lack of motivation to learn and immoral behavior" (p. 2). For Mexican Americans, deficit thinking has been used to explain low achievement in school and to shape policies and school conditions for them.

Deficit thinking has been used to portray people as abnormal, substandard, and the cause of their own inferior status in society. Though the deficit model focuses on individual weaknesses, it has also been linked to assumed group weaknesses, in particular, a focus on the alleged weaknesses of racial/ethnic minorities and the poor. Within this framework, the disadvantaged position of entire groups of people was thought to be easily understood and attributable to their own group deficiencies. Early deficit research went so far as to examine the possibility that racial minorities were not human. Additionally, pseudoscientific craniology studies sought to link the alleged larger brains of Whites to their superiority as a race (Menchaca, 1997). While these early forms of deficit thinking may seem far-fetched and outlandish by contemporary sensibilities, forms of deficit thinking continue to influence dominant narratives around Mexican Americans and low achievement in school.

Two types of deficit thinking models have been used to understand the low academic achievement of Mexican American students: genetic and cultural deficit. Genetic deficit thinking was based on the premise of an innate and unchangeable deficit that stemmed from the biological makeup of a person. The focus was on the assumption that there was something wrong or lacking in the genes of these people that affected their **cognitive** and intellectual abilities, resulting in their low status in society. For Mexican Americans, mixed racial heritage had long been singled out as the cause of assumed intellectual inferiority. A combination of racial heritages resulted in Mexican Americans being referred to as mestizo (mixed blood). These have included Indigenous, European, and African heritages, among others. Of particular focus were the Indigenous and European heritages because Indigenous peoples were considered to be racially inferior, and— among European groups—the Spanish, likewise, were considered inferior. The combination of these two backgrounds for many Mexican Americans was considered a disastrous genetic makeup and thought to explain their low position in society.

Genetic deficit thinking has long been a part of American society but became particularly relevant to education and Mexican Americans in the first three decades of the 1900s, when university scholars and scientists institutionalized this ideology as a legitimate area of study. In this instance, the area of study was intelligence. Intelligence was believed to be an innate ability that was fixed, constant, and unalterable by the environment. That is, it was thought that people were born with a specific level of intelligence that could not be developed. From 1900 to the 1930s, hundreds of research studies were conducted to compare racial/ethnic group differences in physical and intellectual attributes. In 1916, prominent psychologist and intelligence testing proponent Lewis Terman (1916) noted about Mexican Americans: "Their dullness seems to be racial, or at least inherent in the family stocks from which they came" (as cited in Valencia,

1997b, pp. 61–62). Valencia (1997b) identified eight research studies from the 1920s using intelligence tests that included Mexican American participants. In all eight of these studies, the authors concluded that the lower test performance of Mexican Americans compared to their White peers was due to inferior genetics or heredity. Based on results such as these from intelligence tests, Gonzalez (1974) estimates that about 50 percent of Mexican American children in Los Angeles were placed in classes for students labeled as "mentally subaverage" and "mentally retarded" in the late 1920s (as cited in Valencia, 1997b). Therefore, based on intelligence tests, which were presumed to be objective and legitimate, the idea of the innate intellectual inferiority of Mexican Americans was substantiated and served as justification for providing unequal educational opportunities.

The ideas of innate intelligence and testing for intelligence fit well with the mood of the country in the early twentieth century toward social efficiency. Social efficiency was the idea that American society could and should be more efficient for the political and economic development of the country. Part of being more efficient meant developing an educational system that could accurately sort and prepare students for their future roles in a **stratified** labor market. As noted earlier, intelligence tests showed Mexican American children to be "inferior" in intelligence due to their low scores. This placed them at an educational disadvantage in school and justified segregation, their placement in rooms for supposedly slow and disabled learners, and the provision of curriculums that prepared them for low-skill and menial jobs.

The second type of deficit thinking used to understand the low academic achievement of Mexican American students was cultural. Cultural deficit thinking focused on the deficiencies and dysfunction of a culture as the cause of the group's inferior position in society. Using cultural deficit thinking, many scholars and school leaders have presumed that Mexican American cultural values have been detrimental to their social mobility. Thus, the cultural values of Mexican Americans have been studied, labeled as deficient, and used to explain their low achievement in the educational system.

These assumed deficient values of Mexican Americans included present versus future time orientation, immediate instead of deferred gratification, an emphasis on cooperation rather than competition, and placing little value on education and upward mobility (D. G. Solórzano & Solórzano, 1995). These values were considered opposite to presumed middle-class Anglo American values and, therefore, considered detrimental to progress in American society. Within the framework of cultural deficit thinking, the supposed Mexican American value of living for today without regard for future consequences exhibited irresponsibility and a lack of concern for themselves and their children. The presumed value of cooperation instead of competition was believed to hold them back in education because of insufficient self-centeredness and individual concern and effort. In addition, cultural deficit thinking assumed that Mexican American culture did not value education, and many people used the low achievement of Mexican American students in school as evidence to support this assumption.

Cultural deficit thinking promoted a caricatured view of Mexican Americans as an irresponsible and ignorant people whose own cultural characteristics impeded their educational progress in society. In the 1960s, cultural deficit thinking influenced educational policies and programs set up to address the so-called cultural deficiencies of poor and racial/ethnic minority groups. Operation Head Start (a preschool program) and other compensatory federal educational programs were developed to fill in the gap of academic and social skills presumed to be absent in specific groups. Mexican Americans participated in many of these programs, including those constructed to address their so-called language deficits.

Historically, genetic and cultural deficit thinking dominated **discourse** about Mexican Americans and low achievement in school, influencing unequal treatment and low expectations of them. In the context of deficit thinking, segregation; training for manual, industrial, or domestic labor; placement in "slow learner" classes; and high dropout numbers for Mexican American students seemed to not need further investigation and perhaps even appeared justified.

Although acceptance of genetic and cultural deficit thinking has risen and fallen over the years, both types of thinking remain. The debate about the genetic basis of intelligence and its affect on school achievement patterns resurfaced in the 1990s with Herrnstein & Murray's (1994) publication of *The Bell Curve*, which reasserted a genetic basis for differences in IQ among racial groups. More recently, there was also controversy over the doctoral dissertation of a Heritage Foundation policy analyst (Richwine, 2009) who argued that Latino immigrants (and most likely their children and grandchildren) generally have lower intelligence than native White Americans due to social conditions and genetics. In the dissertation, Richwine proposes restricting groups with low intelligence levels with a more selective immigration policy due to presumed resulting negative economic consequences for American society. Thus, an immigration policy based on his recommendations would curtail Latino immigration due to the belief in their genetic deficiency.

Cultural deficit thinking also continues to affect contemporary discourse but is currently reframed to focus on presumed lack of parental values and involvement in education, lack of a family and home environment that prepares children for academics, and "at risk" students' characteristics (e.g., single-parent homes) (Valencia & Solórzano, 1997). In addition, there remains a common sentiment that Mexican American and other Latino students are simply not as motivated and "naturally" smart as White and Asian American students, in particular. What contemporary genetic and cultural deficit thinking have in common is a belief that discrepancies in educational achievement are due to genetics or some form of cultural inadequacy.

History of Mexican American Schooling

The history of Mexican American schooling has included both educational mistreatment and community struggle for equality of opportunity. This is not to deny that educational progress has been made over time. Mexican Americans have benefited from the increased focus on education in the United States over the twentieth century. Nevertheless, a persistent gap in achievement with their White peers remains. This section highlights important conditions that have impeded educational mobility and spurred action by Mexican American communities. What follows is not a comprehensive overview of the history of Mexican American schooling but a focus on major themes that have characterized this history: segregation, Americanization programs, and community actions. These themes, while not exclusive of each other—in fact, they are intertwined—are presented in this chapter separately, to give a focused discussion of each.

Segregation: Mexican Rooms and Mexican Schools

Historically, a major condition of Mexican American public schooling has been that of segregation. Segregation and exclusion have been a part of American public schools since they first began. However, segregation was legally **institutionalized** in schools with the 1896 case of *Plessy v. Ferguson*. In this case, the Supreme Court of the United States mandated that "separate but equal" public accommodations be upheld for Whites and Blacks. This meant that racial segregation was legal in public facilities, including schools. However, since the Treaty of Guadalupe in 1848, which resulted in the annexation of large portions of Mexico by the United States, the racial classification of Mexican-origin people has been ambiguous; only Mexicans considered to be White were to be granted U.S. citizenship. Most mestizos, Christianized Native Americans, and afromestizos were given inferior political rights (Menchaca, 2001). For Mexican Americans, the lack of legal clarity resulted in changing racial classifications. For example, Texas courts in 1897 ruled that Mexican Americans were White *enough* although not truly White (Gomez, 2007). In California, they were considered White, but in the early 1930s attempts were made to reclassify them as "Indians" in order to segregate them legally by race in school (Donato, 1997). By 1935, the California school code allowed segregation for Mexicans of "Indian" descent but not "White" Mexicans (Menchaca, 1995). In general, most Mexican Americans were considered racially "mixed" or "mongrel" and, thus, non-White and second class for social and political purposes, including maintaining segregated schools.

Nevertheless, segregation was never nationally legally mandated for Mexican Americans as a specifically identified group. Local school boards, however, used the power of the state to create educational policies that segregated Mexican American students in public schools (see Donato and Hanson, 2012, who argue that these local policies should now be viewed as legal mandates for racial segregation or **de jure segregation**). Many scholars have concluded that for Mexican Americans, school segregation was not accomplished legally on racial grounds but on educational grounds. The argument by school boards and leadership was that Mexican American students needed separate facilities and instruction due to a variety of factors including language and culture (Donato, 1997; Gonzalez, 1990).

The segregation of Mexican American students has been a critical component of schooling in the American Southwest. Segregation took place in two forms: Mexican rooms (also called "foreign classrooms") and Mexican schools. Mexican rooms segregated Mexican American students from White students in classrooms within the same school; Mexican schools were entire schools exclusive to Mexican American students. Scholars have noted that while segregated schools existed in the United States before 1848, the number of schools exclusively for Mexican American students increased dramatically after 1870 due to "popular demands, legal mandates, increasing financial ability, and a greater acceptance of the ideal of common schooling by local and state political leaders" (San Miguel Jr. &

Valencia, 1998, p. 4). By the 1880s, superintendent of public instruction Chaves (1892) noted that more than 50 percent of school-age children in New Mexican territory (the majority of them of Mexican origin) were enrolled in segregated schools (as cited in San Miguel Jr. & Valencia, 1998). By 1930, South Texas had a 90 percent segregation rate for Mexican Americans (Montejano, 1987). By the mid-1930s, Gonzalez (1974) found that 85 percent of school districts in the Southwest were segregated in some form. The extent of segregation varied by state: the south Rio Grande Valley in Texas segregated most grades up to high school, while smaller school districts in California varied the grade level in which segregation ended (as cited in Gonzalez, 1990).

Although the federal court case *Plessy v. Ferguson* mandated separate but equal public facilities for Whites and African Americans, segregated schools for African Americans were never equal. Likewise, neither were segregated schools for Mexican Americans. Most segregated Mexican schools were overcrowded and in poor condition, lacked proper school equipment, and had poorly trained teachers, especially as compared to schools for White students (Donato, 2007; Menchaca, 1995; San Miguel Jr., 1987). For example, San Miguel Jr. (1987) noted that while rural Tejano (Texas Mexican) children in the 1800s were discouraged from attending schools by landowners, some public schools, known as rancho schools, were in poor condition and lacked resources. He notes:

> The rancho schools were unsightly and lacking in equipment and in properly trained staff. In some South Texas counties the rancho school buildings were jacales, thatched-roofed huts with dirt floors. There were neither blackboards nor desks of any kind; the children wrote on slates and sat on crude backless benches or boxes. (p. 12)

Additionally, Menchaca's (1995) analysis of Santa Paula, California, schools in the mid-1920s found that the schools for Mexican-origin students were inferior to the schools for White students. She found that Canyon School, built for Mexican-origin students, and Isbell School, built for White students, differed in size, amenities, and even construction materials (see figures 1 and 2).

Menchaca notes that Canyon School was constructed of wood and had eight classrooms for about 950 students. In contrast, Isbell School was constructed of concrete and had twenty-one classrooms for fewer than 700 students. Additionally, Isbell School had an auditorium, a cafeteria, a

Figure 1. The segregated Canyon School for Mexican-origin students. Source: Courtesy of Research Library, Museum of Ventura County.

Figure 2. The segregated Isbell School for white students. Source: *The Mexican American Outsiders: A Community History of Marginalization and Discrimination in California* by Martha Menchaca, Copyright © 1995. By permission of the University of Texas Press.

training shop, and several administrative offices; Canyon School had two bathrooms and one administrative office. A bungalow was moved to Canyon School to serve as the cafeteria a few years after the school was built.

Many of the teachers at Mexican American schools included both novices and teachers banned from other schools for incompetence. Teachers at Mexican American schools were paid less and were "promoted" by moving to White schools (Gonzalez, 1990, 1999). Working at Mexican American schools was a transitory experience exemplified by low pay and low status for teachers, resulting in an unstable teaching force of inexperienced and incompetent staff. Additionally, Mexican American schools tended to have White teachers who were not focused on making connections with students' communities and, thus, were disconnected from Mexican American daily life outside of school.

Scholars have identified several reasons why Mexican American students were segregated, including culture and racism, language, perceived intelligence, and economic and political control. First, educators and school officials argued that it was in the best educational interest of Mexican American students to be separated due to their culture and race. This cultural argument was based on the assumption that Mexican American culture was inferior to Anglo American culture. Mexican American culture, viewed as backward in relation to Anglo American middle-class standards, was believed to reduce their ability to learn. Moreover, according to proponents of segregation, it was also a way of purportedly "shielding" Mexican American students from the psychological damage of being culturally different from White students and from feelings of inferiority for not being able to compete with them academically. In fact, some educators argued that Mexican American children were happier in segregated schools (Wollenberg, 1978).

Additionally, it was argued that segregation would ensure that White students would not be negatively influenced or "held back" by Mexican American students (Donato, 1997; Menchaca, 1995). It was considered to be in the best interest of both communities for schools to teach Mexican American students the morals they were presumed to be lacking, such as honesty and respect for public property, as well as about health and sanitation issues. The Report of Illiteracy in Texas (1923) stated, "There is but one choice in the matter of educating these unfortunate [Mexican] children and that is to put the 'dirty' ones into separate schools til they learn how to 'clean-up' and become eligible to better society" (as cited in Montejano, 1987, p. 228).

The **ideology** of Anglo superiority was an important basis of continued support for separate schools. In the 1930s, one school official noted
on segregating Mexican children, "We segregate for the same reason that
the southerners segregate the Negro. They are an inferior race, that is all"
(Taylor, 1937, as cited in Delgado Bernal, 2000, pp. 70–71). Public pressure by Whites was instrumental in creating school district zones that kept
Mexican American students in segregated schools (Delgado Bernal, 2000;
Wollenberg, 1978).

In addition to cultural and race-based rationales, the dominance of
the Spanish language among most Mexican American students was
also considered a detriment to their ability to learn and, thus, also supported segregated school facilities. Many school leaders used language as
the stated reason for the necessity of segregated schools; however, many
English-speaking Mexican American children were also segregated. Language difference was often the main rationale used by school officials to
maintain segregation in **desegregation** court cases (discussion forthcoming).

A third rationale used to support segregation was based on intelligence
tests (IQ tests) showing that Mexican American students scored well below
the average for White children. Based on IQ tests, it was claimed that the
alleged "lower mentality" of Mexican Americans precluded their ability to
think abstractly and required separate instruction geared toward this academic limitation. As prominent psychologist Lewis Terman (1916) argued
about Mexican Americans, "Children of this group should be segregated
in special classes and be given instruction which is concrete and practi-
cal. They cannot master abstractions, but they can often be made efficient
workers, able to look out for themselves" (as cited in Valencia, 1997a, pp.
61–62). To many, including school administrators and educators, segregated instruction due to differences in intelligence made educational sense.
Thus, Mexican American boys were prepared for their presumed future
jobs as manual laborers (e.g., shop and metal-work classes) and Mexican
American girls for domestic jobs and their role as housewives (e.g., laun-
dry, cooking, and sewing instruction) (Gonzalez, 1999).

A fourth rationale for maintaining segregated schools was based on economic and political reasons. In order for White community elites and local
growers to maintain economic and political dominance, an uneducated
and undereducated population of cheap labor was needed. There was a
general attitude that too much schooling for Mexican Americans could
potentially "overeducate" workers away from farm and other manual jobs.

In some communities, school attendance laws were not enforced for Mexican American children and migrant children were prohibited from attending school. Therefore, education policies supporting segregated instruction corresponded with political and economic interests (Donato, 1997, 2007; Gonzalez, 1990, 1999).

Americanization Programs

We have these Mexicans to live with, and if we Americanize them we can live with them. (Los Angeles school superintendent statement to district principals; Dorsey, 1923, as cited in Gonzalez, 2000, Americanization section, para. 57)

Americanization programs have also been a central theme in the history of Mexican American schooling. With non-Anglo native-born and immigrant groups from various parts of the world already in the country after the American Revolution, and more continuing to immigrate to the United States, a fear of what a multitude of cultures, languages, and values would mean for American society began. For many, a diversity of cultures, races, and nationalities was considered threatening and potentially destructive to the development and prosperity of the United States. Therefore, for many politicians and school officials, Americanization programs in schools were the logical response to assimilate Mexican-origin children to Anglo American culture and ways of life.

The inculcation and domination of a unified Anglo American culture for both school children and adults was a main goal of Americanization programs. These programs began around the mid-1800s, as thousands of southern and eastern European immigrants flocked to U.S. urban areas. Americanization included both school and community efforts (e.g., adult English classes and political clubs). In schools, Americanization programs were to teach and socialize children to become Americans using an Anglo American mold (Spring, 2011). The curriculum included a focus on teaching English; highlighting positive aspects of the history, politics, and economic system of America (to cultivate patriotism and loyalty); and developing Anglo American standards of righteousness, law, and public decency. Some advocates of these programs believed that if children were taught one language and set of values, American society would have the social cohesion and harmony necessary for the advancement of the country.

Although Americanization programs were provided to many groups of native and immigrant children, these programs were a central aspect of Mexican American schooling. Even though Mexican-origin people were in the Southwest prior to its annexation in 1848, they were viewed as foreigners with a foreign language, culture, and way of life. Americanization policies were seen as necessary by White political leaders and school officials to integrate Mexican Americans into the larger U.S. society. However, not only were Americanization programs driven by the goal of unifying a nation but also by the goal of changing cultures thought to be inferior. From the perspective of Americanization advocates, Anglo American culture was superior, while Mexican American culture was inferior. Some stereotypes of Mexican Americans included characteristics such as dishonesty, proclivity to thievery, immorality, and violence. In a master's thesis by Meguire (1938), she noted that Anglo Americans familiar with Mexicans also believed they were irresponsible, imitative, thriftless, sex-conscious, individualistic, and inclined to procrastinate (as cited in Donato, 1997). Therefore, it made sense to Americanization program advocates to use the school environment and curriculum to attempt to replace the "inferior" Mexican American culture with "superior" Anglo American culture.

The ideological underpinnings of Americanization policies cast Mexican-origin children as problematic. They were viewed as needing transformation in order to be successful in school and American society. Therefore, Americanization also meant **deculturalization** of Mexican American students. San Miguel Jr. (1999) notes that beginning in the 1850s, school policies dictated that English be the language of instruction and discouraged and eliminated the use of Spanish in school. In fact, Mexican American students were punished for speaking Spanish and rewarded for speaking English. Schools also began to eliminate Mexican culture and history in schools by removing Catholic topics and Mexican history textbooks from the curriculum. This was followed in the 1870s to 1890s with a complete prohibition of Spanish in schools. In addition to prohibiting Spanish, Americanization programs for Mexican American students included sanitation practices and work habits (Wollenberg, 1978).

While certainly changing so-called inferior cultures and languages was at the center of Americanization policies, more than anything, Americanization "tended to preserve the political and economic subordination of the Mexican American community" (Gonzalez, 1990, p. 30). In many communities, much of the Americanization curriculum—learning English and developing specific moral and work habits—was for the benefit of employers. Americanization policies did not challenge the status quo of an unequal society but instead maintained it. While cultural and linguistic **assimilation** of Mexican Americans was desired, no change was sought in their low economic and political position and power in the larger society.

Community Action

In addition to segregation and Americanization, a third important aspect of the history of Mexican American schooling was resistance to discriminatory treatment through Mexican American community action. Resistance was exhibited in multiple ways, including legal actions and mobilizations. As discussed earlier in this chapter, Mexican Americans faced many institutional and **normative** barriers in schools (e.g., segregated schools, racist ideologies). However, these barriers did not go uncontested. For example, when in the 1850s public schools began to push out Spanish and exclude or demean Mexican history, many Mexican Americans chose to send their children to secular private and religious parochial schools (San Miguel Jr., 1988). If schools did not exist in their communities, they created their own private schools. In Texas, Tejanos established *escuelitas* (little schools) and ranch schools to provide educational opportunities for their children (De León, 1982; San Miguel Jr., 1987). Many of these schools included a broad and rigorous curriculum and valued bilingualism and biculturalism. Therefore, individual and group efforts by Mexican Americans to combat unequal treatment and increase opportunities in schools are important to note in the history of Mexican American schooling. The following sections discuss desegregation court cases and mobilizations initiated by Mexican Americans and their allies to gain equal educational opportunities.

LEGAL ACTIONS.   There have been a number of legal challenges to unequal conditions for Mexican American students in schools; however, this section highlights only the first desegregation cases. They began in the mid-1920s and were centered primarily in Texas and California but also included lawsuits in Colorado and Arizona. Initially, these cases had only local impact. Eventually, however, some reached the federal level, most notably with *Mendez v. Westminster* (1946), which served as a precedent case for the nationally known school desegregation case, *Brown v. Board of Education* (1954).

The first desegregation case by Mexican Americans was little known. In *Romo v. Laird* (1925), Tempe, Arizona, rancher Adolpho "Babe" Romo

Jr. sued Tempe Elementary School District No. 3 so that his four children would not be required to attend the Eighth Street School. This school, designated by the district for "Spanish-American" and "Mexican-American" children, was a teacher training school and, consequently, used student teachers and not state certified teachers. The **plaintiffs** argued for admission to the better-quality Tenth Street School, which was designated for White students and employed state certified teachers. As in many of the desegregation lawsuits initiated by Mexican Americans that followed, the **defendants** argued that Mexican American students needed to be segregated due to language needs. They claimed that the lack of English proficiency by many Mexican American students necessitated specialized and separate instruction in school, which led to segregation from White students. In his ruling, Judge Joseph S. Jenckes sided with the plaintiffs by ruling that Mexican American students were entitled admission to public school facilities and teachers of the same quality (including state certification) as children of other races. Judge Jenckes ordered that the Romo children (Antonio, Henry, Alice, and Charles) be admitted to Tenth Street School (Muñoz, 2001). While the *Romo* case is significant because it was the first Mexican American–initiated desegregation case, it had little impact beyond the Romo children and the Eighth Street School because it was not a **class action** lawsuit (Valencia, 2008).

In the 1930s, two better-known cases for desegregation followed: *Independent School District v. Salvatierra* (1930) and *Alvarez v. Lemon Grove School District* (1931). Again, defendants in both cases argued that the language needs of Mexican American students necessitated segregated instruction. The *Salvatierra* case was filed in Del Rio, Texas, with the help of the League of United Latin American Citizens (LULAC) on behalf of Mexican American residents and their children, including plaintiff Jesús Salvatierra. *Salvatierra* was important for three key reasons: 1) it forced the courts to determine the constitutionality of segregating Mexican Americans on racial grounds; 2) it served as a basis for future segregation cases; and 3) it allowed LULAC, founded in 1929, to test its powers as an advocacy group (Valencia, Menchaca, & Donato, 2002). The court ruled that it was illegal for the school district to segregate Mexican American students on the basis of race. Although initially the courts restrained the district from segregating Mexican American children, after school district appeals, the Texas Court of Civil Appeals overturned the original ruling. In the appeal, the court found that the district did not arbitrarily segregate students by race; however, based on educational grounds, it did have the authority to segregate students by their need to learn English (Valencia, Menchaca et al., 2002).

Similarly, in the *Alvarez* case in San Diego, California, Judge Claude Chambers ruled that the school board could not segregate Mexican American students based on race and—taking a different position from previous cases—ruled that segregation actually impeded Americanization and learning English for Spanish-speaking children. While the *Alvarez* case was important for being the nation's first successful class action lawsuit against segregation, like previous cases, its influence was strictly local, lacking a national, or even state, impact (Valencia, 2008).

After a lull in desegregation cases by Mexican American plaintiffs after *Romo, Salvatierra,* and *Alvarez,* they resumed after World War II with *Mendez v. Westminster* (1946) and *Delgado v. Bastrop Independent School District* (1948). These cases were significant in that they were the first Mexican American–initiated federal court cases. *Mendez,* another Southern California case, began when Soledad Vidaurri, the aunt of Sylvia, Geronimo, and Gonzalo Jr. Mendez, tried to enroll them in Westminster Elementary School where her own children attended. When she did so, her niece and nephews (of Mexican and Puerto Rican descent) were denied admission to the school. At that time, Westminster Elementary only admitted White children, and she learned that her children had been admitted because of light skin complexions and their last name of French origin. As a result, the Mendez parents and other community parents filed a lawsuit on behalf of their children. *Mendez* was significant because it was the first desegregation case in which the plaintiffs argued that separate school facilities were not equal in K–12 public schools, and, therefore, segregated schools were a violation of the U.S. Constitution's **Equal Protection Clause** of the Fourteenth Amendment.

In the end, Judge Paul McCormick ruled in the *Mendez* case that the defendant school districts discriminated against Mexican-origin students and violated their Fourteenth Amendment rights. Judge McCormick decided that the school board had segregated Mexican American students not on an educational basis but on the basis of "the Latinized or Mexican name of the child" (as cited in Wollenberg, 1978). He also ruled that the board used **gerrymandered** district lines in order to maintain racially segregated schools (San Miguel Jr. & Valencia, 1998). Ultimately, Judge McCormick decided that separate facilities could never be equal because separate facilities would maintain a social inequality that deemed groups superior and inferior in society. As in the *Alvarez* ruling, the judge found no evidence that segregation helped students to develop English proficiency; instead, evidence indicated that it retarded language and cultural assimilation. The *Mendez* case's greatest success was ending de jure segregation in California (Gonzalez, 1990).

Two years later in *Delgado v. Bastrop Independent School District* in Texas, Judge Ben Rice also ruled that the segregation of Mexican American students was discriminatory and illegal and a violation of the Fourteenth Amendment's Equal Protection Clause. However, Judge Rice ruled that schools could segregate first-grade Mexican American students who were not English proficient within integrated schools (Valencia, Menchaca et al., 2002).

While each of these early desegregation cases provided some victories against segregation of Mexican American students, unfortunately, segregation continued and increased. Many school districts did not comply with the court rulings by professing ignorance of the law or refusing to go against local custom and practice of segregation. School districts used the language proviso in many of the rulings as a form of **second-generation segregation** by segregating students by English language proficiency in a single school. In addition, school districts manipulated school district lines and offered only White students the option to choose their school in order to maintain segregated schools despite court-ordered desegregation (San Miguel Jr., 1987). Nevertheless, these first cases demonstrate the desires and efforts of Mexican American parents and organizations to obtain equal educational opportunities for their children. Since these early desegregation lawsuits, Mexican Americans have continued to use the courts to address schooling inequities in the areas of financing, special education, bilingual education, school closures, **undocumented** students, higher-education financing, and **high-stakes testing** (see Valencia, 2008, for a more in-depth discussion of these areas).

MOBILIZING: ORGANIZING GROUPS. As evidenced by early legal actions taken regarding schooling, Mexican American people and communities have not been complacent about the substandard treatment and conditions of their children within the public school system. They were advocacy driven, forming hundreds of parent, student, and community groups and national organizations and using mass demonstration to address the educational issues of Mexican American students. Mexican Americans have a history of organizing groups for the benefit of their communities.

Mutualistas, mutual aid organizations, have been used to help communities pool funds for a variety of needs, including the organization of cultural and political events. Organizations relating to educational issues or advocacy have included—to name just a few—lesser-known neighborhood parent groups such as Comite de Vecinos de Lemon Grove (Lemon Grove Neighborhood Committee, founded circa 1931) and Asociación de Padres de Niños Mexico-Americanos (Parents Association of Mexican American Children, circa 1945); student groups such as Mexican American Student Association (MASA, 1965), Mexican American Youth Organization (MAYO, 1967), United Mexican American Students (UMAS, 1968), and Movimiento Estudiantil Chicano de Aztlan (MEChA, 1969); and well-known advocacy organizations such as the League of United Latin American Citizens (LULAC, 1929), American GI Forum (AGIF, 1948), Brown Berets (1967), National Council of La Raza (1968), and Mexican American Legal Defense and Educational Fund (MALDEF, 1968).

MOBILIZING: SCHOOL WALKOUTS. Many Mexican American student and community demonstrations against inequitable school conditions occurred in the last century. These included one early twentieth-century and two well-known civil rights–era demonstrations: the 1910 San Angelo Walkouts, the 1968 East Los Angeles Walkouts, and the Crystal City Walkouts of 1969 (see Alanis, 2010, for a Chicago-area walkout). These walkouts have also been referred to as blowouts and boycotts. In the 1910 Walkouts in San Angelo, Texas, Mexican American parents boycotted segregated schools due to inferior physical facilities and quality of instruction. Parents demanded their children be allowed to attend the schools White children attended. They argued that while they were contributing taxes to the city, their children were being subjected to segregated and inferior educational conditions. The president of the school board responded that integration of Mexican-origin and White students in the same schools would be a "terrific blow" and "demoralizing" to the entire school system and refused to consider integrated schools (De León, 1974). Mexican American parents in San Angelo formed a committee and hired a legal team to pursue integration. Their demands were largely ignored by the school board, and segregation was upheld. The determination of the Mexican American community was evident in that the boycott of public schools, though not without problems, lasted about five years, ending in 1915. The opening of Mexican Presbyterian Mission School in late 1912 helped sustain the boycott because it was open to all Mexican-origin students and taught a rigorous curriculum. In the end, the boycott was not successful in achieving integrated and equal schooling opportunities for Mexican American students but showed the determination of the Mexican American community to advocate for equity in their children's education (De León, 1974).

Two large-scale and widely known mobilizations by Mexican American communities against educational inequities occurred in the late 1960s. The 1960s was an era of heightened political action and demonstration across the nation. During this period, people of color and women were calling attention to discriminatory practices and making demands to end them in many institutions of society, including schools. For Mexican Americans, these demands for change were part of a larger civil rights and **Chicano movement**. In the 1968 East Los Angeles Walkouts, over 10,000 students walked out of five predominantly Mexican American high schools, motivated by poor educational conditions and the fact that previous attempts for school change by the community had been ignored. The demonstration lasted approximately a week and a half, and participants included not only high school students but college students, teachers, and other community members (Delgado Bernal, 1998). The students made many important demands of the school board, including offering bilingual and bicultural education; more focus on Chicana/o history and folklore; smaller class sizes; better guidance counseling; improved student-counselor ratios; ending the sorting of students into slow, average, and high ability using flawed IQ tests; building new schools and destroying condemned buildings; expanding library facilities; providing more materials in Spanish; and ending corporal punishment, among others (McCurdy, 1968). Several meetings with the school board allowed student strikers and their supporters to present their concerns and demands. In the end, the school board argued that there was little they could do to meet students' demands. They argued that while they agreed with 99 percent of the students' demands, due to financial reasons they could not implement the massive changes requested (McCurdy, 1968). Nevertheless, the walkouts and the larger Chicano movement served as inspiration for continued mobilizations for Mexican American equality.

A second large-scale mobilization against educational inequity occurred in Crystal City, Texas, in 1969. The initial impetus for the Crystal City Walkouts was the rejection by Mexican American students of the new process for selecting school cheerleaders. As the population of Mexican American students increased in the high school, the process was changed from being student elected to faculty selected. The unofficial quota system used by a faculty committee of selecting three White cheerleaders to one Mexican American cheerleader was not acceptable to Mexican American students (Shockley, 1974). Equally unacceptable was a new requirement for the homecoming sweetheart to have one parent be a high school graduate, which effectively locked out the majority of Mexican American girls. This led to a series of events where students demanded input into their schooling conditions and challenged discriminatory practices.

At a school board meeting in November 1969, Mexican American students of Crystal City submitted a list of demands that included giving the student body power to elect their own school representatives, including cheerleaders and sweethearts, and limiting teacher control in these matters. Student demands also included incorporation of bilingual and bicultural education, an advisory board for the school administration made up of Mexican American community members, educating teachers about Mexican American culture, and hiring more Mexican American teachers. They also demanded that "teachers should not call students names like, animals, stupid idiots, and ignorants" (as cited in Shockley, 1974, p. 233). After all student demands were rejected at a December 9, 1969, school board meeting, the students of Crystal City, Texas, called for a boycott. More than 1,700 students, with parental and community support, successfully boycotted until school let out for Christmas break on December 19 and continued to rally and meet through the holiday break. Additionally, three student leaders flew to Washington, DC, at the invitation of Texas senator Ralph W. Yarborough and other federal government officials, including those from the Department of Justice, to inform them of the plight in Crystal City schools and seek their intervention (see figure 3) (Gutiérrez, 2005). On January 7, 1970, after several meetings between a negotiating team representing the boycotting students and the school administration, the school boycott was called off after school board members approved most of the students' demands.

As previously discussed, the history of Mexican American education has included segregation and Americanization programs. The emphasis in school was on separation due to alleged difference and inferiority. The need to change the language and culture of Mexican American students was seen as necessary, both so that they could be considered suitable for any interactions with the larger society but also so that the supposedly negative linguistic and cultural attributes of Mexican Americans would not

Figure 3. Student walkout leaders Mario Treviño, Severita Lara, and Diana Serna in Washington, DC, with Senator Ralph Yarborough to discuss educational conditions in Crystal City, Texas, December 18, 1969. Source: Courtesy of Diana Serna Aguilera.

permeate the larger society. Nevertheless, the history of Mexican American education has also included resisting unequal conditions in schools through the American court system; forming parent, student, and community organizations; and mass demonstration.

Reproduction and Other Frameworks

While historically deficit thinking has been the lens through which Mexican Americans and their schooling experiences have been viewed, this perspective has not gone unchallenged by Mexican Americans, other communities of color, social justice allies, and academic scholars who have developed alternative lenses. Frameworks and ways of interpreting the social world do not emerge in isolation but are rooted in prior frameworks and narratives of a historical and social context. The following perspectives partially developed in response to—and to challenge—deficit thinking and to fill in gaps in understanding schooling and society. The premise of deficit thinking— that there was something genetically or culturally wrong with a person or group—has been challenged by frameworks that seek to understand the role of power, social status, and various forms of oppression in American society. The next sections emphasize academic frameworks and discourse since the 1960s that bring new understandings of academic achievement and schooling experiences. Of the many frameworks and strands, this section only briefly discusses select trends in the research on Mexican American education.

Reproduction Theories

One major theoretical framework that developed as a social critique was social reproduction (see Bowles & Gintis, 1976, and Bourdieu & Passeron, 1977, for seminal works). This theoretical framework was based on a Marxist perspective of inherent and constant social class conflict in a capitalistic society between dominant classes (owners/capitalists, upper social classes) and subordinate classes (workers/laborers, low social classes). In this framework, the dominant classes continuously attempt to take advantage of and control the subordinate classes in order to maintain control of the social, economic, and political spheres of society. The dominant classes do so by the use of force, manipulation, and promotion of ideologies that support acceptance of an unequal society and their dominance.

Using a Marxist perspective, scholars began to look at school as an institution that reproduced inequalities in society by preparing students of different social classes for different jobs in the labor market. Schools were viewed as a means for dominant classes to maintain control. From a social reproduction perspective, schools were not benign or neutral institutions but set up to benefit the "haves" (middle and upper class) in society and repress the "have nots" (working class and poor). Schools were structured to reproduce labor market and economic inequalities in society so that the dominant classes maintained their social, economic, and political privileges. Schools served as a mechanism to sort students, based on their class background, into different occupations for a highly stratified labor market: middle and upper social classes for semiprestigious and prestigious and well compensated professions and low social classes for low-paid and low-skill jobs. For the low social classes, this was done by providing inferior schooling conditions such as insufficient and inferior resources (e.g., lack of supplies and unqualified teachers) and an unchallenging curriculum that only prepared students with the knowledge, attitude, habits, and skills for low-skill jobs.

One way the dominant classes were believed to be able to accomplish this was through control of dominant discourse about school in society. A major component of this discourse was the normalization of the achievement ideology, which was the idea that success in school was primarily determined by individual efforts. Also normalized was the idea that schools were equal and an avenue of upward mobility for everyone in society regardless of social class. Therefore, if a person worked hard in school, he or she could achieve academic success. By promoting belief in the achievement ideology, the dominant classes secured their power because subordinate groups would accept the idea that the schooling system was fair and that failure in school was due to lack of effort or will to succeed. Thus, the ideology supported the view that the lack of mobility of subordinate groups was their own fault. For social reproductionists, the achievement ideology promoted the myth of equal opportunity in school, which served to placate disenfranchised classes from resisting an unequal school system and allowed the dominant classes to maintain control.

Similar to social reproduction, the theory of cultural reproduction also viewed schools as reproducing inequality in society. The focal point, however, was on how the **cultural capital** of the dominant classes was recognized and rewarded in school, while that of subordinate classes was excluded and devalued. In fact, the cultural capital subordinate classes brought to school was considered a hindrance and disadvantage for academic success. Valued cultural capital included knowledge, skills, attitudes, and experiences that middle- and upper-class children inherited from their parents. For example, upper-class etiquette or speaking style taught at home or knowledge of other countries acquired by travel would be cultural capital used as indicators of intelligence and academic success. Therefore, children of the dominant classes were able to succeed academically due to possession and normalization of their parental cultural capital, while those of the subordinate classes found academic success difficult due to lack of the "right" cultural capital (see chapter 5 for further discussion).

Critiques of social and cultural reproduction theory have been numerous. One major critique was that reproduction theories viewed social class as the exclusive source of conflict and cause of inequality in society. Due to this emphasis, reproduction theory was viewed as too deterministic—that the social class structure was so powerful that low–social class children were unequivocally doomed to academic failure and upper- and middle-class children destined to academic success. Other strands of research have argued that social statuses in society, such as race, ethnicity, and gender, also play a role in maintaining an unequal society. Additionally, other theorists have put more focus on **human agency** and the view that humans are not simply puppets to be manipulated in a class-divided society; they are capable of taking actions to resist oppressive circumstances or pursue their own agendas.

Since reproduction theory first emerged, various other theoretical frameworks and lines of research have been used to examine Mexican American schooling experiences. An in-depth discussion of the numerous theories and research is not the intended goal of this section; however, it is important to note that these frameworks introduced new lenses through which to understand the low achievement of Mexican American students, historically and contemporarily. While certainly never accepted by all, the dominance of genetic and cultural deficit thinking was challenged and refuted by these perspectives.

Critiques of Power: Critical Theory, Critical Race Theory, and Chicana Feminism

Many theories have attempted to address some of the criticisms of reproduction theory, such as the roles of human agency, race/ethnicity, and gender in the processes and social relations of schools. These include critical theory, critical race theory, and Chicana feminism (more detail on each of these in chapter 5). Unlike reproduction theory, critical theory views schools as sites where power struggles between dominant and disenfranchised classes take place, and people (students, parents, and teachers) are able to resist oppressive conditions. Moreover, if subordinate classes and educators develop *conscientização* (a critical consciousness discussed in chapter 5), they are able to actively work to change these conditions.

Critical race theory (CRT) and Latina and Latino critical race theory (LatCrit) in education consider race a central factor in school and also acknowledge that it intersects with other forms of subordination such as social class, gender, and sexual orientation. These theories also reject the idea that schools provide equal opportunity and are committed to social justice by attempting to abolish racism and other forms of oppression.

Chicana feminism highlights and values the strengths of Chicanas based on their diverse lived experiences. In the school context, Chicana feminism critiques the institutions that exclude or marginalize the culture, knowledge, and experiences of Chicanas. This theory focuses on the forms of resistance Chicanas use to navigate and succeed in school, despite oppressive conditions.

Critical Ethnography

Some theoretical frameworks (such as those just discussed) also emphasize learning about schooling experiences and conditions by listening to the very people who experience oppression in school. Listening to "average" and marginalized people counters traditional academic research that typically relies on so-called experts to analyze and make conclusions about Mexican Americans and instead respects and values the insight and experience of Mexican Americans, regardless of social position. By centering the voices of Mexican American people and communities, it is believed that much insight can be gained from their perspectives about schooling. Moreover, an emphasis on the "lived experiences" of Mexican Americans in understanding school achievement generated a research method called critical ethnography. This method recognizes that society consists of groups with differing levels of economic and political power. By centering those with limited power, critical ethnography incorporates voices previously silenced or devalued in society into the dialogue about schools or other sectors of society. Numerous important works on Mexican Americans in the last few decades have used this research method (e.g., Ochoa, 2004, 2013; Valenzuela, 1999; Valdés, 1996).

Unequal School Conditions

Some research in education has attempted to explain low academic achievement (some research grounded in the theories just discussed), especially for poor students and students of color, by focusing specifically on analysis of unequal school conditions. This research focuses on inadequate funding of schools, inferior resources, school organization, ability grouping, curriculum tracking, low expectations, and less experienced or highly transient teachers at urban, impoverished, and racially segregated schools. This research attributes the poor achievement of Mexican American students to inferior school conditions. Chapter 2 discusses in more detail research that examines racial segregation and curriculum tracking as factors resulting in unequal school conditions for Mexican American students.

Contemporary Educational Achievement Indicators

So far, this chapter has examined important aspects of Mexican American schooling: deficit thinking models used to understand and explain low educational achievement, negative school conditions and community mobilizations against them, and contemporary frameworks seeking to understand various ideologies and factors affecting Mexican American schooling. With that context, this section turns to the contemporary academic achievement of Mexican American students by examining several indicators of educational attainment to provide an overall perspective of their status.

Many types of educational indicators are used to assess students' educational progress. Some common indicators used to assess progress in elementary and secondary education include test scores, grade delay, push-out rates, and high school graduation rates. For college, these may also include application, attendance, entrance exam scores, and graduation rates. Over the last forty years, Latino students have improved on many of these indicators. For example, Carter and Wilson (1997) found high school completion rates for Latinos from 1975 to 1995 improved from 38 percent to 53 percent (as cited in Valencia, 2002a). Although the bulk of improvement in the push-out rate has occurred in the last decade, nevertheless, the push-out rate for Latinos also improved from 1972 to 2010, lowering from about 34 percent to about 15.1 percent (Aud et al., 2012; National Center for Education Statistics, 2001). Some of the progress is reflective of educational gains for all racial/ethnic groups since the 1970s. Nevertheless, even with improvements over time, a persistent gap between Mexican American and non-Hispanic White students on many educational indicators has not changed. The achievement gap with White students has been a focal point for much of the research on Mexican American educational attainment, and yet the processes fostering these gaps continue largely unaddressed (see Ochoa, 2013). These contributing processes (e.g., segregation, curriculum tracking) are discussed in later chapters.

Figure 4 illustrates the educational pipeline for Mexican American students and reveals many problematic areas. Using 2009 U.S. Census data, Covarrubias (2011) shows a likely educational pathway for one hundred Mexican American elementary school students. He writes of those initial one hundred students,

> 44% of students entering the educational pipeline are eventually pushed out before completing a high school diploma. Of the remaining 56% who graduate from high school, 27 will enroll in college, some going to community college and others enrolling in 4-year universities. We find that of the 27 who move on to college, 5 will terminate their educational journey having earned

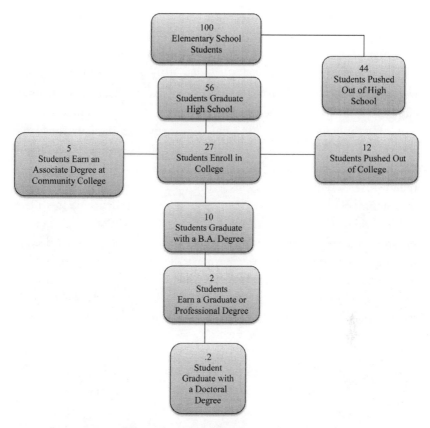

Figure 4. The Chicana/o educational pipeline showing graduation outcomes for Chicana/o elementary school students. Source: Adapted from Covarrubias (2011), figure 1.

only an associate's degree, whereas 10 will earn a baccalaureate. Still, of those who enter college, 12 (44%) will be pushed out prematurely, having earned no degree. Of the 10 with a bachelor's degree, only 2 will earn a graduate or professional degree, and an insufficient .2 will earn a doctorate. (p. 92)

From figure 4, it is evident that large portions of Mexican American students do not make important transitions, especially graduating from high school, enrolling in college, and graduating from college with a bachelor's or advanced degree. Other research using the pipeline approach shows that of Chicana/o students who go to community college only about 6 percent (one of seventeen) transfer to a four-year university (Yosso, 2006). Thus, a critical transition is not being made by many students who start at a community college. These findings support other research documenting that

Mexican American students achieve less at various points in the educational pipeline, especially when compared to other racial/ethnic groups (Fry, 2002, 2005; Rumberger & Rodriguez, 2011; Valencia, 2002b).

The **National Assessment of Educational Progress** (NAEP) provides information about the reading and math scores of Hispanic students in comparison to White students. Table 1 shows national average reading scores for students in fourth and eighth grades by race/ethnicity. The table shows a gap in scores between Hispanic and White students in both grade levels. Hispanic students scored twenty-five and twenty-two points lower than White students in fourth and eighth grades, respectively. A similar gap in mathematics scores between Hispanic and White students is also evident in NAEP data (not shown here).

Dropout and graduation rates are other important indicators reflecting the educational status of Mexican American students. Dropping out has long-term economic consequences that include limited future job prospects and lifetime earnings, which can be from about a quarter to one-half million dollars less than a high school graduate. Table 2 shows dropout rates by race/ethnicity.

Table 1. Average Reading Scale Scores, by Race/Ethnicity and Grade, 2011

	GRADE 4	GRADE 8
White	231	274
Hispanic	206	252
Black	205	249
Asian/Pacific Islander	235	275

Source: Snyder & Dillow, 2013, table 142

Table 2. High School Dropouts Among Persons Sixteen to Twenty-Four Years Old, by Race/Ethnicity, 2007

	STATUS DROPOUT RATE (%)
White	6.1
Mexican	22.2
Black	11.5
Asian	3.0

Note: Status dropout rate is the proportion of persons in an age group who have not completed high school and are not enrolled in school, regardless of when they dropped out.
Source: Aud, Fox, & KewalRamani, 2010, table 18.1b

The total dropout rate among sixteen- to twenty-four-year-old Mexican-origin youth is more than triple the rate for Whites: 22 percent compared to 6 percent, respectively. More than one in five Mexican American youths is pushed out of high school. This can partially be attributed to differences between those born in the United States and those born outside the United States. Native-born Mexican American youths have a 12 percent dropout rate, compared to non–native born at 38.8 percent (Aud, Fox, & KewalRamani, 2010). Nevertheless, native-born Mexican Americans still have a dropout rate double that of White youths.

Among Latino subgroups age twenty-five years and older, Mexican Americans fare among the worst. U.S. Census data have shown that Mexican Americans and Central Americans had a 45 percent dropout rate compared to 20 percent for Cubans, 24 percent for Puerto Ricans, and 14 percent for South Americans (Rumberger & Rodriguez, 2011). As with the younger cohort discussed in the previous paragraph, these high push-out rates for Mexican Americans and other Latino groups among those age twenty-five and older are partially attributable to a large number of foreign-born (or nonmainland for Puerto Ricans) persons in these populations, some who never attend U.S. (or mainland) schools. In addition to dropout rates, the graduation rates of Hispanic and White students also reflect a disparity. Table 3 shows the graduation rate at about 68 percent for Hispanic high school students, compared to about 85 percent for White students.

The gap with White youth in primary and secondary education indicators extends to college indicators as well. Table 4 shows that among twenty-five to twenty-nine-year-olds, the percentage of persons with a

Table 3. Averaged Freshman Graduation Rate (AFGR), by Race/Ethnicity, 2011–2012

	AFGR (%)
White, non-Hispanic	85.0
Hispanic	76.0
Black, non-Hispanic	68.0
Asian/Pacific Islander	93.0

Note: Averaged Freshman Graduation Rate is an estimate of the percentage of an entering freshman class graduating in four years.
Source: Stetser & Stillwell, 2014, table 4

Table 4. Bachelor's or Higher Degree Among Persons Twenty-Five to Twenty-Nine Years Old, by Race/Ethnicity, 2007

	% BACHELOR'S OR HIGHER DEGREE
White	32.6
Mexican	8.5
Black	17.2
Asian	59.6

Source: Aud, Fox, & KewalRamani, 2010, table 27b

bachelor's degree or higher was about 8.5 percent for Mexican-origin adults, compared to about 32.6 percent for Whites.

These educational indicators provide a snapshot of the contemporary position of Mexican Americans in the educational pipeline. While there has been improvement over time on many of these indicators, persistent gaps remain between Mexican American and White students, a continued focus of scholars, schools, and the media. These gaps are the outcomes of various social, economic, and political inequalities in the American school system. Working toward understanding the causes of these achievement discrepancies and developing solutions to address them will help to bring about the sustained academic success of Mexican American students, their communities, and American society as a whole.

Concluding Thoughts

U.S. schools represent the essence of the American dream: equal opportunity for upward mobility. While schools have provided upward mobility for many Americans, they have also perpetuated inequalities from the larger society. The schooling history of Mexican-origin people in the United States has been characterized by limitations on their academic opportunities, hostility toward their culture and the Spanish language, and resistance to discriminatory and unequal schooling conditions. This chapter discussed deficit thinking and how it has been used to explain the low achievement of Mexican American students and limit the kinds of schooling opportunities afforded them. The so-called mental dullness of Mexican American students was used to provide them with classes for "slow" students and courses that prepared them for menial jobs. Deficit thinking affected the educational opportunities afforded Mexican American students and has had a lasting legacy in terms of how they have been viewed and treated academically.

This chapter also provided an overview of the context for unequal schooling. Segregation and Americanization programs have played important roles in shaping Mexican American students' schooling experiences. Nevertheless, while the educational system structured the learning conditions for Mexican American students, Mexican Americans resisted negative conditions in school repeatedly and in a variety of ways.

Critical contemporary theories on education move away from blaming Mexican American genetic makeup and culture to provide alternative frameworks for understanding their schooling. These include the view of schools as institutions that reproduce inequalities from the larger society, a focus on unequal school conditions, and the role of oppressive systems such as racism and sexism. Finally, contemporary indicators of academic achievement show an achievement gap on a variety of educational indicators for Mexican Americans in comparison to their White peers. Many concerned persons and groups seek to understand the reasons for this gap and work toward creating a schooling environment that addresses these issues and provides just educational conditions and experiences.

Discussion Exercises

1. Discuss the depiction of Mexican Americans (e.g., values, characteristics) based on genetic or cultural deficit thinking. How do you think this depiction affected their schooling experiences historically? Do you think genetic or cultural deficit thinking affect Mexican American schooling today?

2. List the ways that segregated schools affected educational opportunities for Mexican American students. Brainstorm other kinds of impacts that segregated schools may have had on them.

3. Why were Mexican Americans viewed as needing Americanization programs? Discuss the affect of Americanization programs on Mexican American students and their relationship with school.

4. Why were legal actions and mobilizations necessary to get equal educational opportunities for Mexican Americans? How were these strategies different from and similar to each other?

.5. How is reproduction theory different from deficit thinking? Are these differences important? Why?

6. Choose two tables of contemporary educational indicators from this chapter to examine (e.g., reading scores, dropout rates). Develop a list of potential reasons for the gap between Mexican Americans and Whites for these indicators. What can be done to address these factors?

Suggested Readings

Donato, R. (2007). *Mexicans and Hispanos: In Colorado schools and communities, 1920–1960*. Albany: State University of New York Press.

Gonzalez, G. G. (1990). *Chicano education in the era of segregation*. Philadelphia: Balch Institute Press.

Menchaca, M. (1995). *The Mexican outsiders: A community history of marginalization and discrimination in California*. Austin: University of Texas Press.

Moreno, J. F. (1999). *The elusive quest for equality: 150 years of Chicano/Chicana education*. Cambridge, MA: Harvard Educational Review.

San Miguel, G. (1987). *Let all of them take heed: Mexican Americans and the campaign for educational equality in Texas, 1910–1981*. Austin: University of Texas Press.

Valencia, R. R. (2008). *Chicano students and the courts: The Mexican American legal struggle for educational equality*. New York: New York University Press.

Valencia, R. R. (2011). *Chicano school failure and success: Past, present, and future* (3rd ed.). London: Routledge.

Chapter 2

School Barriers to Academic Success in K–12

"She's really smart, and so she did well in school."

"He really worked hard and got into a good college."

"He never really liked school, so he ended up dropping out."

"Es burra. No le entra nada." (tocándole a su hija la cabeza) ("She's a dummy. Nothing enters." [knocking on her daughter's head])

The above statements typify comments heard regarding students and their abilities, efforts, and motivation in school. They serve as easy explanations to understand why some students are successful in school, while others are not. They also reflect American society's emphasis on individual characteristics or efforts to explain educational success and failure. For Mexican American students, low academic achievement is often blamed on a lack of motivation and effort in school, which is assumed to stem from familial and cultural values. While individual achievement, effort, and motivation are critical factors for educational success, other factors also affect an individual's educational trajectory. When professional educators, social scientists, or researchers who study educational achievement find that social behaviors such as either being pushed out of high school or graduating affect social groups differently (e.g., wealthy students versus poor students), and that there are discernible patterns to how they affect social groups, they look beyond an exclusive focus on individual characteristics and may also examine larger historical, institutional, and social factors affecting those groups. Some factors that have affected Mexican Americans' schooling were discussed in the previous chapter. This chapter focuses on a few contemporary institutional factors that impede educational mobility for Mexican American students: segregated schools, educational testing, and curriculum tracking. While these factors are intertwined, each is discussed separately.

Segregation Continues

While segregation is a documented part of the history of Mexican American schooling (although not widely known), it is often overlooked as a contemporary issue affecting Mexican American students. Segregation is commonly regarded as a historical phenomenon addressed by the 1954 Supreme Court case *Brown v. Board of Education of Topeka* that outlawed segregation in public schools. Due to this well-known decision made about sixty years ago, the impact of segregation on contemporary public schooling is not generally recognized as problematic. In reality, even with this landmark case, segregation did not proceed quickly. One year later, with *Brown v. Board of Education of Topeka* (1955; known as *Brown II*) school districts challenged the original ruling, and, consequently, the Court gave the power of implementing desegregation to local district courts with the vague wording of "with all deliberate speed." For communities staunchly against desegregation, especially in the South, this allowed them to resist and stall integration for a decade or more. Nevertheless, due to these nationally known court cases, segregated schools are not viewed as an important factor currently affecting Mexican American students. However, despite the end to legal segregation in public schools, segregation is a critical contemporary issue for Mexican Americans. In fact, for Latino students, segregation has been *increasing* in recent decades, and these students are significantly more segregated than African American students in suburban areas (Orfield, Frankenberg, Ee, & Kuscera, 2014; Orfield & Yun, 1999).

After the *Brown* and *Brown II* decisions and the Civil Rights Act of 1964, desegregation of public schools became a federal issue in education. While Mexican Americans had been using local, state, and federal courts to combat segregation since the mid-1920s, it was these federal actions that began to address this issue on a national level. For Mexican Americans, *Cisneros v. Corpus Christi Independent School District* (1970) in Texas and *Keyes v. School District No. 1* (1973, 1975) in Denver, Colorado, were important legal precedents affecting the desegregation process by recognizing Mexican Americans as an identifiable minority group that could benefit from *Brown*. Before these cases, Mexican Americans had legally been considered "other white," and, therefore, pairing Mexican Americans and African American students in the same schools was being used in some instances to technically comply with desegregation orders. However, the *Cisneros* and *Keyes* cases removed this loophole to resist integration of White students with African American and Mexican American students (Valencia, Menchaca et al., 2002). Even with important court rulings that specifically incorporated Mexican Americans into desegregation efforts, there was never significant enforcement of desegregation rights for Latinos (Orfield, 2001), and educational isolation continued in both segregated and desegregated public schools (Valencia, Menchaca et al., 2002).

Increasing Segregation

The segregation of Latinos has been steadily increasing in American public schools (Orfield, Bachmeier, James, & Eitle, 1997; Orfield et al., 2014). This **resegregation** has intensified throughout the nation to a point of **hypersegregation**. Beginning in the early 1970s, a series of court cases sought to challenge desegregation orders (e.g., *Milliken v. Bradley*, 1974). The affect of these court cases was not immediate; however, by the late 1980s, a litany of cases reversed prior desegregation orders throughout the nation by releasing school districts and cities from desegregation plans.

The Civil Rights Project has documented a continued trend over several decades toward intensified segregation of Latinos (Orfield, 2001; Orfield et al., 1997; Orfield et al., 2014; Orfield & Lee, 2007; Orfield & Yun, 1999). Based on their analyses of national data, table 5 shows the percentage of Latino students on two measures of segregation from 1968 to 2005: students who

Table 5. Latino Students in Predominantly Minority and Minority Schools, by Selected Years

	PERCENTAGE LATINO IN PREDOMINANTLY MINORITY (OVER 50%) SCHOOLS	PERCENTAGE LATINO IN MINORITY (90%–100%) SCHOOLS
1968	55	23
1980	68	29
1988	74	33
2005	78	39
Percentage Change 1968–2005	+23	+16

Source: Orfield & Lee, 2007, tables 16 and 17

attended predominantly minority (over 50 percent minority) schools and students who attended minority (90 percent to 100 percent minority) schools. Over this thirty-seven-year period, the data show the percentages of Latinos attending predominantly minority and minority schools increased steadily. The data show that the percentage of Latinos attending predominantly minority schools increased by 23 percent (from 55 percent to 78 percent). Therefore, in 2005, almost eight out of ten Latino students were attending predominantly minority schools. On the second measure of segregation in table 5, data from the Civil Rights Project show that the percentage of Latino students attending a 90 percent to 100 percent minority school increased by 16 percent (from 23 to 39 percent). Therefore, in 2005, about four out of ten Latino students attended a minority school with 10 percent or less White students.

Analysis by the Civil Rights Project also shows evidence on a third measure of segregation, the Latino/White exposure index, of intensifying segregation over three decades (see figure 5). This measure of segregation looks at all of the schools in the nation and determines the average percentage of White students in a school attended by a typical Latino student. In 1970, a typical Latino attended a school with about 44 percent White students, but in 1998 this was down to 29 percent White students. Continuing the downward trend, in 2011–2012 (not shown in table) an average Latino went to a school with about 25 percent White students (Orfield et al., 2014). Therefore, on all three measures of segregation, data show

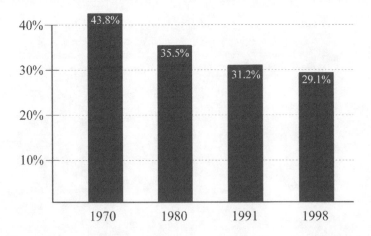

Figure 5. Percentage of White students in schools attended by typical Latino students, by selected years: 1970–1998. Source: Adapted from Orfield (2001), table 10.

a clear trend toward increasing racial/ethnic segregation for Latino students, which indicates significant racial isolation and less contact with non-Latino White students.

Research also shows that increased Latino school segregation is not uniform across the nation. State data show that California, New York, and Texas are consistently among the top three states on all three measures of segregation (Orfield & Lee, 2006). In two of these states that rank highly for school segregation of Latinos—California and Texas—Mexican Americans are the majority Latino group.

Factors Contributing to Increasing Segregation

Several factors may have contributed to the intensified segregation of Latino students in the last few decades. One factor is the growth of the Latino population in the United States and the resulting increase in public school enrollment. According to U.S. Census Bureau data, from 1980 to 2010 the population of Latinos in the United States increased from 14.6 million to 50.5 million (Ennis et al., 2011; Gibson & Jung, 2002). The Mexican American population has increased 54 percent in the last decade alone (2000–2010) (Ennis et al., 2011). In addition, public school enrollment of Latinos has increased 380 percent from 2 million to 9.6 million students from 1968 to 2005 (Orfield & Lee, 2007). Today, Latinos make up almost one out of four public school students (National Center for Education Statistics, 2013). A second factor that may have affected school segregation is increased residential segregation for Latinos. Latinos are concentrated in metropolitan areas in a few states (although there has been more dispersion in the last decade). Many are also economically limited in their choice of where to live, and thus, residential segregation persists. A third factor that may have led to increased segregation is the lack of federal support for desegregation. While the public at large views integration as beneficial, since the 1970s the federal courts have moved away from supporting desegregation efforts (Orfield & Lee, 2006). Federal courts have chosen to release districts from court-ordered desegregation and busing orders, resulting in the weakening of federal desegregation efforts.

Segregated Schools and Low Academic Achievement

The benefits of integrated schooling are often thought to primarily focus around the idea of promoting interracial interaction and harmony. While this is an important goal, a more fundamentally democratic goal has to do with providing equitable educational opportunities to all students. Segregated schools are related to inferior education and poor academic achievement (Orfield et al., 1997; Valencia, 2011b). On various measures of academic achievement—including test scores, push-out rates, graduation rates, and college entrance exam attempts and scores—attending racially segregated schools has negative consequences. For example, Valencia (2011b) found in several Texas school districts that as the percentage of Latinos and African Americans increased in schools so did the failure rate on the state high-stakes test Texas Assessment of Knowledge and Skills (TAKS). In the same study, a strong association was found between the percentage of Latinos and African Americans in San Diego, California, schools and dropout rates. National research confirms this pattern. Balfanz and Legters (2004) found that in 2002, almost one-third of the high schools that were more than 50 percent minority graduated less than half of their class. In addition, one-half of predominantly minority schools had drop-out rates over 40 percent, as did two-thirds of the schools with less than one-tenth White students (as cited in Orfield & Lee, 2005). Finally, racially segregated schools are more likely to have larger class sizes and less likely to have qualified and experienced teachers.

Segregation and Concentrated Poverty

One critical reason for the negative effects of racially segregated schools on academic achievement is the high concentration of students living in poverty in these schools. Intensely segregated Latino schools face **double segregation** by both race and socioeconomic situation. **Concentrated poverty** is a fundamental difference between minority segregated schools and White segregated schools. Minority segregated schools are much more likely to have concentrated poverty than White segregated schools (Orfield et al., 1997; Orfield et al., 2014). More than 80 percent of African American and Latino intensely segregated schools face conditions of concentrated poverty as compared to 24 percent of White segregated schools. Additionally, in 2005–2006, the average Latino student attended a school where almost 60 percent of the students were poor (Orfield & Lee, 2007). This has serious implications because research has shown a strong relation between concentrated poverty and low academic achievement (Orfield et al., 1997; Orfield et al., 2014). High rates of poverty in schools are associated with low academic achievement on important indicators such as test scores, graduation rates, and college attendance. In addition, schools with concentrated poverty have fewer high-achieving students and a less stable and qualified teaching staff.

Schools with concentrated poverty are also likely to exist in communities with multiple distress factors outside of the school. These include housing inadequacy, violence, unemployment, drug abuse, and other crimes. Additionally, high-poverty schools are likely to serve high numbers of students with nutritional and health needs, which affects students' abilities to concentrate and learn. Each of these distress factors in a community affects schooling for the students who live in them.

Addressing Racially Segregated Schools

Racially segregated schools need to be recognized as unequal educational opportunities that affect all races and have implications for American society as a whole. The problem of racially segregated schools is a complex one, and, therefore, ideas about how to resolve increasing segregation are also complex and multifaceted. Given the large numbers of Latino students affected by segregation and the negative implications of attending racially segregated schools, it is imperative to move toward desegregating schools. How can American society concretely move toward desegregating schools? The following is an abbreviated version of five policy recommendations Orfield and Lee (2007) put forward to address the current trend of increasing racial segregation in schools:

- Attack housing segregation, which is the root of many forms of racial inequality, including segregated schools.

- Communities still under court desegregation orders should exercise caution in ending those orders because their rights to address racial separation might be taken away.

- Where desegregation plans are forbidden by a court, local school authorities should do what they can to pursue other forms of diversity such as geographic, linguistic, and SES [socioeconomic status] diversity.

- Choice programs [such as magnet schools and charter schools] should be operated in ways that support integration as much as possible.

- Congress needs to act. The major breakthroughs in race relations have followed congressional actions to require and/or support racial progress.

Valencia, Menchaca et al. (2002) and Valencia (2011b) make some of these same recommendations (e.g., residential segregation, need for Congress to act) but also developed some recommendations that specifically address Mexican American segregation. First, community case studies need to be conducted in order to understand the origins and persistence of school segregation. This information could be used in court cases to show how past segregation affects current school segregation. Second, court-ordered busing programs used to desegregate schools (which have been largely discontinued) must be reinstated. Busing minority children to their school worked to maintain class desegregation for Latinos in Denver, Colorado, until the courts released the district from mandatory busing in 1995. Third, Mexican Americans and African Americans need to build coalitions to work on many school issues that affect both groups—including segregation. Fourth, Mexican Americans have not had, and need, representation on school boards. Representation would provide necessary political power to advocate for the needs of Mexican American students. Fifth, expanding the use of two-way bilingual education (discussed in chapter 3 as dual-language immersion) could help to reduce language segregation by integrating both English- and Spanish-dominant students in a learning environment where bilingualism is valued. Finally, teacher education programs need to incorporate critical theory (discussed in chapters 1 and 5). Critical theory can help future teachers develop critical perspectives of schooling, which can lead to questioning, debunking of myths, critiques of traditional schooling practices and pedagogies, understanding power dynamics in schools, and advocating for socially just schools.

Educational Testing

Educational testing for Mexican American students is a topic of great interest and concern due to how tests have been and are being used in American public schools. *Educational testing* is a broad term that includes a variety of tests, including intelligence tests, behavioral and psychological tests, achievement tests, and high-stakes tests. Although a dominant opinion on tests is that they are objective and fair methods of evaluating student achievement, many scholars and communities of color have questioned their use and fairness. As discussed in chapter 1, supposedly scientifically based and objective intelligence tests have been used to classify and label Mexican American students as having low levels of intelligence. As a result, they were provided limited educational and occupational opportunities. While educational tests may have had legitimate roles in school, they have also served an abusive function. In the last decade, an increased entrenchment of the ideology of accountability and a singular focus on using **standardized tests** to assess student achievement in American public schooling has raised concerns about harming and disadvantaging Mexican American students.

There are several concerns about the current dominance of standardized testing and high-stakes tests in public schools. One concern is the overreliance on one form of assessing students (primarily standardized "bubble-in" tests) and the repudiation of research showing that students learn in different ways and should be assessed in different ways. Another concern is that learning can become narrowed if the content of and preparation for state and national tests becomes the overriding focus in the classroom. Learning the "correct" answers for these tests may come at the expense of learning more broadly and deeply (beyond memorization). Teachers may deemphasize subjects not being tested (e.g., history and music), alternative ways of thinking about and responding to an issue, and the development of critical-thinking and problem-solving skills. Finally, standardized tests may perpetuate societal inequalities. As Kornhaber and Orfield (2001) state, "Since tests tend to measure unequal backgrounds and opportunities, and not simply an individual's effort, negative consequences are more likely to affect black, Hispanic, and poor youths than they are to affect those whose families and schools offer the richest preparation" (pp. 1–2). Thus, for Mexican American students, a largely lower-middle class, working-class, and poor economic status affects their achievement on standardized tests.

Due to the relationship between student background and educational testing, a primary concern is that Mexican Americans score lower (as a whole) on most standardized tests than non-Latino White students, resulting in negative consequences at various points in the educational pipeline. For example, as shown in chapter 1, the National Assessment of Educational Progress (NAEP) shows that Latino students consistently score below their White peers in reading (see table 1 in chapter 1). Although NAEP scores for Latinos have improved since the 1990s, the gap in achievement with White students has persisted. The gap in scores on NAEP is representative of the gap that occurs on many educational tests. This means that in a public school system that relies heavily on standardized tests to assess student abilities, and that serves as gatekeeper for grade promotion, graduation, and college entrance, many of the negative repercussions of low scores fall on Mexican American students and schools with large Mexican American student and English learner populations.

Problems with Educational Testing for Mexican Americans

Valencia (1999) and Valencia, Villarreal, and Salinas (2002) have identified six issues surrounding educational testing that are pertinent to Mexican American schooling (see figure 6). First, the **cultural bias** of intelligence tests used in special education diagnosis has not been fully understood, and much more research in this area is needed. Research that specifically examines special education children has not taken place, and some of the most prominently used intelligence tests have been underexamined regarding cultural bias. Unfortunately, recent trends show a reduced level of research on cultural bias of intelligence tests instead of more scrutiny. Second, assessing limited English proficient (LEP) students is problematic because they are not assessed for language dominance, fluency, and proficiency before given intellectual or academic assessments in English. In addition, LEP students are not properly assessed prior to entering and exiting bilingual programs and bilingual special education. Thus, the risks for LEP students include incorrect assessment (e.g., diagnosis of a language disorder) and/or premature exit from bilingual programs into mainstream English classes. Third, because school districts rely heavily on high IQ scores or other types of aptitude or achievement tests to access Gifted and Talented Education (GATE), Mexican American students are **underrepresented** in these programs. In addition, the lack of assessing

1.	Potential cultural bias of tests for special education
2.	Problems in assessment of Limited English Proficient students
3.	Underrepresenatation in Gifted and Talented programs
4.	High-stakes tests have become gatekeepers to educational mobility
5.	Overrepresentation in middle and low curriculum tracks
6.	SAT has limited college access

Figure 6. Problems with educational testing for Mexican Americans. Source: Valencia (1999).

English language proficiency of Mexican American students remains an issue in testing for GATE.

A fourth issue identified by Valencia as problematic is that using high-stakes tests for promotion and high school graduation has become a gatekeeper for educational mobility for Mexican American students. Using high-stakes tests as the sole determiner of a student's ability to graduate is problematic because test scores represent a small sample of behavior and should always be used with other forms of assessment. Fifth, because standardized tests play an important role in determining what type of curriculum students have access to (e.g., remedial, honors), curriculum tracking (or curriculum differentiation) disadvantages Mexican American students with unequal learning opportunities. Being disproportionately placed in non–college bound curriculum tracks affects teacher quality, self-esteem, and access to high-status knowledge—that is, the knowledge and skills needed for getting into and succeeding in college. Sixth, the use of the Scholastic Aptitude Test (SAT) has adversely affected admissions to institutions of higher education for Mexican American students. Mexican Americans consistently receive lower scores than White students on both the verbal and math portions of the SAT, affecting whether and where they can attend college. While curriculum tracking is discussed in more detail in the next section, what follows is a more specific discussion on three areas noted as problematic for Mexican American students due to standardized testing: gifted education, special education, and high-stakes testing.

GIFTED EDUCATION. Gifted students of color have been called the "neglected of the neglected" (Valencia & Suzuki, 2001). Despite increased research on gifted students, there has been very little research on students of color in gifted programs. What *is* known is that Latino students are underrepresented in gifted programs (Valencia & Villarreal, 2011; Valencia, Villarreal et al., 2002). U.S. Department of Education, Office of Civil Rights (2008) data show that Latino students are 1.9 times less likely than White students to be identified as gifted. Additionally, Latino students are underrepresented nationally in gifted programs (37.3 percent) and in the four states with the largest population of Mexican Americans, California, Texas, Arizona, and Illinois (as cited in Valencia & Villarreal, 2011).

An important issue in Mexican American underrepresentation in gifted programs is that assessment of giftedness has been traditionally based on intelligence tests. Giftedness is thought to be captured by high scores on IQ tests. Thus, for Mexican American students who on average score lower than their White peers on IQ tests, chance for admission to gifted programs is reduced. Additionally, because English proficiency is emphasized in the identification of gifted students, many English learners are probably not even considered for gifted programs until after they become English proficient (Valencia, Villarreal et al., 2002). Finally, while many scholars criticize the very notion of giftedness as elitist and **socially constructed**, nonetheless, Mexican American underrepresentation in gifted programs denies access to enriched curriculum and resource opportunities and is considered a form of second-generation segregation.

SPECIAL EDUCATION. Contrary to underrepresentation in gifted programs, Latinos are overrepresented in special education programs. However, the overrepresentation is not consistently visible; examining the overall rate in special education nationally, Latinos are not overrepresented. They are, however, overrepresented in specific states, high-poverty areas, minority-concentrated areas, and specific subcategories of special education (Artiles, Waitoller, & Neal, 2011; Rueda, Artiles, Salazar, & Higareda, 2002). For example, according to the U.S. Department of Education (2000), they are overrepresented in the categories of specific learning disability, hearing impairments, and orthopedic impairments (as cited in Rueda et al., 2002).

Assessment for special education is an area of concern for Mexican American students. Similar to gifted programs, the continued use of IQ tests in the definition and assessment for special education has also raised concerns about cultural and linguistic bias. Additionally, testing conducted exclusively in English is problematic for proper assessment of many Mexican American students. Research has shown that children of immigrant Latinos have a higher chance of being identified as disabled and low achievement in English (reading, oral, comprehension), a common reason for their referral to special education (Rueda et al., 2002). With the elimination of bilingual education in some states and national emphasis on standardized testing in English in recent decades, the affect on referrals and assessments of Mexican American students (many linguistic minorities or English learners) to special education is of continuing concern.

The overrepresentation of Latinos and English learners placed in special education is problematic because there is no guarantee students are receiving quality services (e.g., enriched individualized educational support, high-quality tutoring) that will improve their academic achievement or outcomes (Rueda et al., 2002). In fact, research has shown that Latino students' IQ scores tend to decrease after receiving services in special education programs. Therefore, even with improvements in the last few decades in the assessment of Mexican American and other students of color, problems persist in their placement in special education.

HIGH-STAKES TESTING. While various types of educational tests have been used in public schools since their inception, since the 1980s there has been a movement toward high-stakes testing. High-stakes testing has been defined as

> the exclusive or near-exclusive use of a test score to make significant educational decisions about students, teachers (prospective and incumbent), and schools. Such decisions can have desirable or undesirable consequences for students, teachers, and schools. That is, a great deal rides on the results of certain tests. A significant gain or loss can result from test score outcomes (hence the notion of high-stakes). (Valencia & Guadarrama, 1996, p. 562)

Among the significant negative effects of high-stakes tests are placement in low-curriculum tracks, grade retention, and denial of a high school diploma. The use of high-stakes testing is part of a "get tough" philosophy that proponents argue will motivate students, teachers, and schools to strive harder and, thus, improve education. Critics, however, argue that high-stakes testing does not motivate students to work harder but instead discourages them and does not improve the quality of education. Critics further argue that high-stakes testing creates additional barriers for already vulnerable student populations, including Mexican Americans and other students of color, low-income students, and English learners.

Research has shown that high-stakes testing has an adverse effect on Mexican American students. These students are not passing high school exit exams at the same rate as their White peers and, as a result, not receiving high school diplomas. Approximately one-half of U.S. states currently use high school exit exams, which research has shown have a negative impact on the academic progress of Latino students and English learners. For example, the California High School Exit Exam (CAHSEE) (begun in 2002 but not fully implemented until 2006) has consistently shown racial/ethnic and English proficiency discrepancies in pass rates. At its start, the pass rate for Latino students was about 84 percent, while for White students it was about 97 percent. For English learners (who are predominantly Latino students), the outcome was worse: one in four students did not pass the exam (Mehta, 2006). For the class of 2013, rates have improved, with about 94 percent of Latino and 99 percent of White students passing the CAHSEE. For English learners, the pass rate was 82 percent (Human Resources Research Organization, 2013, table 2.11). However, these may be overestimates because these percentages do not include students who did not pass and did not continue trying or those who left school before the end of tenth grade (when testing begins).

In Texas, where high-stakes grade promotion and high school exit exams have been used since the early 1990s, Latino students have also not fared well. Papers filed in the federal court case *GI Forum v. Texas Education Agency* (2000) showed an adverse impact of the Texas Assessment of Academic Skills (TAAS) on students of color. Lead attorney for the Mexican American Legal Defense and Education Fund Albert Kauffman (1999) reported that in 1997, 87 percent of all students who failed the TAAS high school exit exam were either African American or Latino (as cited in Valenzuela, 2005). Despite a disparate impact of TAAS on students of color, the court in *GI Forum* ruled that a state had the power to design an educational test it felt best met the needs of its citizens. Additionally, data from the Texas Education Agency (2003) show that 79 percent of English-proficient Latino students in third through eighth grade and tenth grade passed the exam, compared to 92 percent of White students. English learners, largely Spanish speaking, had a 58 percent pass rate (as cited in McNeil, 2005). While TAAS is no longer in use, it has been replaced with the Texas Assessment of Knowledge and Skills (TAKS) (and most recently the State of Texas Assessments of Academic Readiness [STAAR]), which has also shown lower pass rates for Latino students in comparison to White students.

Scholars who have studied the effects of high-stakes tests argue that this centralized testing focuses the curriculum on test preparation with the sole goal of raising test scores, particularly in low-income and minority-dominant schools. The result is more class time and school resources allocated to test preparation, reducing tested subjects to basic information and skills and relegating untested subjects to marginalization. Thus, instead of improving learning, the instruction's quality and quantity is severely compromised (McNeil & Valenzuela, 2001).

In 2002, the largest nationwide high-stakes testing initiative was signed into law: No Child Left Behind (NCLB). NCLB is the reauthorization of the Elementary and Secondary Education Act (ESEA) of 1965, which provided federal funds targeted to address the needs of low-income students, English learners, and students with special needs. NCLB changed many aspects of the ESEA, most notably by institutionalizing a form of nationwide testing. NCLB mandates annual assessment in grades three through eight in reading and math and less frequent assessments on science. Although, theoretically, states can opt out of testing, realistically they cannot afford to lose the federal funding tied to it. Additionally, states are required to report student assessment by subgroups, including race/ethnicity, gender, English proficiency, economic disadvantage, and disability status. Schools are held accountable to reach specific benchmarks (called adequate yearly progress) overall and for each subgroup. NCLB is part of the standards-based school movement that equates testing with educational accountability and equity (by having the same standards for all students). Therefore, if a school does not reach the designated benchmarks, the school is classified as "in need of improvement," and, if adequate progress is subsequently not made, the school faces possible state takeover or closure.

In the last decade, NCLB has affected Mexican American students in many ways. First, test scores correlate to family income; thus, belonging to a large working-class and poor population puts Mexican American students at risk for punishment for low achievement on the yearly assessments. Because standardized tests such as NCLB are assumed by top school officials and politicians to be unbiased, the student groups who achieve low scores are considered the problem. Second, Mexican American students are more likely than White students to attend impoverished and segregated schools and schools with more English learners and students with special needs. These factors put them at risk for being in schools labeled as failing due to low achievement and suffering the punitive consequences of being in a school designated as such. Top education officials assume that schools with specific characteristics (high poverty) are "equalized" to a degree with superficial extra resources. Therefore, it is considered "fair" to compare students and schools and punish those who do not do well or do not improve. Third, if school districts and schools feel immense pressure to raise test scores, the students considered to be problematic (due to low scores) may be pushed out of school. Finally, because NCLB is modeled after TAAS (the state standardized test formerly used in Texas), which showed gaps in achievement by race/ethnicity, the risk of a persisting gap in achievement between Mexican American and White students is likely.

Recommendations for Equitable Schools and Accountability

In the last few decades, American public schools have been moving toward increased use of standardized testing and standards-based school reform. Proponents of this movement have argued that these reforms will improve students, teachers, and schools because each will be held accountable for their results (student test scores). This is based on the rationale that good results (high test scores) will be rewarded and bad results will be punished, and these incentives will drive educational standards upward and improve the quality of education. However, critics of standards-based reform argue that this system simply "treats the *symptoms* (i.e., low academic achievement) rather than the *cause* (i.e., inferior schools, unequal educational opportunity) of racial/ethnic differences in academic achievement" (Valencia, Villarreal et al., 2002, p. 294; italics in original). Since students from impoverished or low-income families and communities, those attending segregated schools, and English learners are more likely to score low on achievement tests, they bear the brunt of the negative repercussions of standardized testing.

Critics of standards-based reform claim not to be against accountability or testing. They are simply against how tests are being used and the idea that a single test score is adequate for assessing students' academic achievements. They do not equate accountability with standardized or high-stakes testing. Valencia (1999) provides suggestions for improving the educational testing of Mexican American students. First, alternative forms of intelligence assessment (used in GATE and special education evaluations) need to be developed and evaluated. Second, English learners need to be assessed properly in their English abilities before given intellectual or academic achievement tests. Third, testing should move away from sorting and labeling students and toward monitoring student achievement. Educational testing should be used to learn how to improve schools, by identifying students' strengths and weaknesses. Finally, student assessments should use multiple measures. Using multiple assessments that incorporate tests, parent and teacher informants, classroom observations, and medical records provides valuable information and improves the credibility of that information.

Critics also argue that the standards-based reform movement has been largely a top-down initiative. Politicians, government officials, and others not directly involved in education have imposed reforms that affect students, parents, educators, and local communities across the nation. Critics argue that it is these latter constituents who are left voiceless in the push for accountability. Speaking specifically about Texas's state accountability system, which was touted as a model for the nation, Valenzuela (2005) also argues that accountability promotes a subtractive approach to educating racial, cultural, and linguistic minorities. She writes:

> Children, along with their parents and communities, are treated as objects. The very notion of a mainstream, standardized educational experience implies a systematic disregard of children's personal, cultural, and community-based identities. Rather than providing children with an empowering sense of how their lives can connect productively to the world that they inhabit, a test-centric curriculum compelled by the long arm of the state through standardized, high-stakes testing reduces children's worth to their test scores. (p. 4)

Therefore, standardized testing, when overemphasized and heavily weighted in assessing students, can be disadvantageous if not used appropriately and in conjunction with other forms of assessment.

Curriculum Tracking: Within-School Segregation

A third institutional factor that affects Mexican American schooling is curriculum tracking (or curriculum differentiation). Curriculum tracking is a form of within-school segregation that has negatively affected the educational experiences and opportunities of Mexican American students. It is also referred to as second-generation segregation because it can occur within integrated or racially mixed schools. Curriculum tracking is "the process whereby students are divided into categories so that they can be assigned in groups to various kinds of classes. Students are classified as fast, average, or slow learners and placed into fast, average or slow classes on the basis of their scores on achievement or ability tests" (Oakes, 1985, p. 3). In elementary school, the sorting of students is called "ability grouping" and may be used for math and reading. In high school, students may be sorted or tracked into classes referred to as advanced placement, honors, college prep, regular, or remedial, among other classifications. A central differentiating factor between these courses is that some prepare students for college and provide an academically rigorous curriculum, while others do not. The courses for students not considered college-bound may instead focus on teaching basic skills, working specifically toward high school graduation, or preparation for semiskilled work immediately after high school. Curriculum tracking is not only a contemporary phenomenon but, as discussed in chapter 1, has historically stunted the educational opportunities of Mexican American students by sorting them into industrial and low-rigor curriculum. Unfortunately, curriculum tracking continues to stunt the educational opportunities of Mexican American students.

In American society, sorting students by perceived ability is viewed as a "natural" way to structure schooling, and curriculum tracking is viewed as beneficial to all students, including those considered fast, average, and slow learners. However, alternative perspectives challenge classifying students as such and view curriculum tracking as harmful. Critics of curriculum tracking view it as a socially constructed hierarchy that maintains and creates benefits for students considered fast learners and disadvantages students considered average or slow. That is, views of children as slow or fast learners are determined through biased school mechanisms (i.e., tests) and negatively affect those at the bottom of the hierarchy. Research has shown that a student's track can affect various educational outcomes, including cognitive tests in math, science, reading, and writing; the likelihood of high school graduation; and expecting to attend, applying to, being accepted to, and graduating from college. High-track placement (e.g., advanced placement, honors) benefits students, while low-track placement disadvantages students on these outcomes (Ballón, 1999; Gamoran, 1987; Gamoran & Mare, 1989; Oakes, Gamoran, & Page, 1992). In addition, curriculum tracking stratifies students by race/ethnicity and social class background and, thus, reinforces segregated groupings. Unfortunately, because Mexican Americans have not been considered fast learners or high-ability students, they have overwhelmingly been disadvantaged in the tracking hierarchy.

Curriculum tracking is an important aspect of Mexican American schooling because studies have consistently shown that Latino students are overrepresented in non–college bound and low tracks (Ballón, 2008; Braddock & Dawkins, 1993; Oakes, 1995; Oakes & Guiton, 1995; Oakes, Selvin, Karoly, & Guiton, 1992; Ochoa, 2013). More specifically, Latino students are more likely to be in non–college bound tracks, such as remedial, vocational, and special education programs, and less likely to be in honors programs or to take advanced placement courses in comparison to their White peers. One study that examined Mexican Americans in the Southwest (Arizona, California, Colorado, New Mexico, and Texas) found that about 68 percent of Mexican American and 66 percent of African American students were in non–college bound math courses, as compared with about 50 percent of White students and 32 percent of Asian American students. Additionally, only about 4 percent of Mexican American students were in honors math compared to about 12 percent each for African American and White students and 27 percent for Asian American students (Ballón, 2008).

Disadvantages of Low Tracks

As in most hierarchical structures, courses in college and non–college bound tracks are not equally viewed, valued, or treated, and neither are the students taking them. There is educational privilege in being at the top of a track system and disadvantage for those at the bottom. In fact, being in a non–college bound or low track can mean inferior educational experiences and opportunities as compared to those in college-bound or high tracks (Oakes, 1985, 1995; Oakes, Gamoran et al., 1992; Ochoa, 2013). Figure 7 summarizes the disadvantages of being in low-track courses.

Some of the disadvantages for students in low-track courses emerge from who teaches the courses, how the courses are taught, and what is taught. Low-track courses are often taught by less experienced teachers and teachers who are less likely to be certified or hold degrees in the subject matter taught (Oakes, 1990). Researchers have also found that low-track courses are taught at a slower pace of instruction, which can result

1.	Less experienced teachers
2.	Less qualified teachers
3.	Slower pace of instruction
4.	Less academically rigorous curriculum
5.	College bound thinking skills not taught

Figure 7. Summary of disadvantages of low-track courses.

in substantial disparities over the course of high school (Oakes, Gamoran et al., 1992). The pace of instruction makes it virtually impossible for low-track students to ever "catch up." Finally, students in low-track courses are taught less academically rigorous material and are not taught the intellectual skills necessary for college, such as critical and analytic thinking and problem solving.

Outside of the classroom, research has also shown differential treatment by track. Students in low tracks have less access to and attention from counselors and are dealt with more harshly for violating school rules in comparison to high-track students (Ochoa, 2013). Therefore, since Mexican American students are overrepresented in non–college bound tracks, they experience many of the disadvantages of curriculum tracking.

Factors Influencing Track Placement

How do Mexican American students end up overrepresented in non–college bound tracks and underrepresented in college-bound tracks? While schools may use a variety of criteria to determine track placement, one of the primary mechanisms used to sort students into tracks is standardized test scores. As discussed in the previous section on educational testing, on average, Mexican American students score lower on achievement tests in comparison to their White peers. Therefore, they often do not meet the criteria for entrance into college-bound tracks. An important issue to remember is that test scores are influenced by social class and race/ethnicity. That is, social class and race/ethnicity affect test scores, and test scores affect track placement. On average, White middle- and upper-class students score better on achievement tests than Mexican American, working-class, and poor students. Middle- and upper-class parents are able to supplement their children's education with tutoring, test preparation classes, and academically enriching programs. Thus, test score discrepancies are due to factors such as social class and cultural test bias and differences in prior schooling conditions and opportunities (including linguistic conditions), among other factors. Nevertheless, tests meant only to measure specific knowledge in a given time frame are often used to make assumptions about students' intellectual capabilities and the pace at which they learn (both assumed to be permanent). Over time, these assumptions and continued curriculum tracking solidify a student's position in the tracking hierarchy.

Despite the strong impact of social class and race/ethnicity on achievement tests, their use in the placement of students into tracks is considered by schools to be a fair and objective way of sorting students. However, what can further skew the sorting process is that it is not uncommon for schools to lack clearly specified criteria for assigning students to tracks and to inconsistently apply them. For Latino students, this ambiguity and inconsistency can be particularly problematic. In a study that examined Latino track placement in school districts in Rockford, Illinois, and San Jose, California, Oakes (1995) found inconsistent use of test scores for track placement for different racial/ethnic groups. Latino students with scores comparable to White and Asian American students were less likely to be placed into high-track classes. The study found that in San Jose, Latino eighth graders with average scores on achievement tests were three times *less likely* than Whites with average scores to be placed in an accelerated math course. Therefore, even though Latino students had comparable scores to students from other racial/ethnic groups, they were less likely to be in high-track classes.

Why would Latino students be tracked differently from their White and Asian peers with comparable test scores? One answer is that teachers and school personnel do not view Latino students the same way they do White and Asian American students (Oakes, Selvin et al., 1992; Ochoa, 2013). Research has found that school teachers and counselors link racial/ethnic groups to particular tracks. More specifically, Asian American students were strongly identified with advanced courses, high motivation, and high tracks, while Latino students were identified with remedial courses, low motivation, and low tracks. This has been referred to as academic profiling (Ochoa, 2013). These racialized perceptions of students' suitability and motivation for particular classes and tracks can influence counselor and teacher assessment and recommendation for student track assignment. Moreover, Mexican American students may also opt out of more rigorous courses if they feel racially isolated or "out of place" in courses where they may be the only one or among the few of their background. If racial/ethnic patterns are evident in a track hierarchy, students of color in high tracks may also question their own academic abilities and feel that their placement in rigorous courses was in error, potentially causing them to move out of these classes on their own.

Another factor that may influence the track placement of Mexican American students is students and their parents who are unaware that curriculum tracking is a form of stratification in schools that strongly influences college attendance. Awareness of the implications of curriculum tracking for college attendance is typical of students whose parents are middle or upper class and college educated. Middle- and upper-class schools are also more likely to have the programs and resources promoting a college-bound culture. Therefore, Mexican American students whose parents are overwhelmingly not middle or upper class and college educated are disadvantaged in not understanding the successful navigation of the educational system and the long-term consequences of track placement. For example, middle- or upper-class parents are more likely to know that specific math courses are needed for college preparation and, thus, are more likely to advocate for their child to be put in these courses. Compounding this, Mexican American students' parents may either have not experienced the U.S. educational system or, even if they did attend U.S. schools, were not in college-bound courses or did not go on to college. Therefore, Mexican American parents are less likely to know that specific classes are needed to prepare for college enrollment and to directly question school personnel about the course recommendations of teachers and counselors for their children. However, even when Latino parents do voice reservations about or opposition to their child's course assignment, school personnel may discourage challenges to their recommendations (Auerbach, 2002).

Another factor that affects the track placement of Latino students is attending racially and socioeconomically segregated schools. Segregated schools offer students fewer opportunities in the college tracks. Mexican American students who may be considered college-bound but attend predominantly minority and poor schools encounter schools with smaller academic tracks, fewer advanced courses, and a less rigorous college preparatory program (Oakes, Gamoran et al., 1992). Even though Mexican Americans with high test scores have a better chance of entry into college-bound classes at these schools, they receive fewer opportunities than students attending a school with large and well-supported college-bound tracks.

Curriculum Tracking Complacency

Even though curriculum tracking affects educational outcomes negatively for students in non–college bound tracks, it is not viewed by the public as an unequal system within schools. Generally, American society does not consider curriculum tracking a form of segregation and educational inequality. It is simply viewed as the way school is organized, and therefore, public scrutiny and criticism are not widespread. Curriculum tracking is not considered problematic for various reasons. First, curriculum tracking is considered by many to be a legitimate, fair, and necessary form of instruction. The mechanisms used to sort students (e.g., achievement tests) and the actual classroom separation of students are viewed as legitimate and justifiable. Thus, the overrepresentation of Mexican American students in non–college bound tracks is not considered by the public or even most school personnel as racial/ethnic, linguistic, or socioeconomic bias or unequal treatment in any way. It is seen as merely a consequence of the use of "objective" criteria, such as standardized tests, to sort students into tracks. A second factor working against Mexican American students specifically is the general perception in American society that they and their families do not value education. A common myth is that Mexican American students do not do well in school because their parents do not care about or support their children's education. This perception allows Mexican American students to be easily faulted for academic disengagement and lack of progress and discourages a critical examination of curriculum tracking and how this system influences opportunities and, ultimately, academic achievement.

Detracking Efforts

While the public at large has not been alarmed by curriculum tracking in school, many civil rights activists, researchers, educators, parents, and other concerned parties called attention in the late 1980s to the detrimental effects of curriculum tracking for low-track students and the disproportionately negative impact on students of color and low SES students. This was followed in the 1990s by calls for reform by **detracking** schools. Detracking is meant to eliminate or reduce the stratified tracking system that labels and sorts students into high, medium, and low tracks. Ideally, low tracks would be eliminated, and all students—including perceived high-, medium-, and low-ability students—would have access to an academically rigorous and challenging curriculum.

Detracking rejects the core values of curriculum tracking that intelligence is unidimensional, innate, and fixed; students naturally fall into high-, medium-, and low-intellect categories; and cultural deficits play a role in achievement gaps. Detracking reforms are based on the idea that intelligence is multidimensional, a social construct, and malleable. That is, there are multiple ways to define and measure students' abilities, and these can be developed and change over time. All students are capable of and entitled to a challenging curriculum, not only a select segment of the student population.

Therefore, a wider range of teaching methods and modes of assessing students is necessary. Detracking principles also reject the notion that intelligence is restricted to certain racial/ethnic or socioeconomic groups, instead arguing that intelligence is manifest equally in all groups.

In the 1990s, some states and school districts either volunteered or were court-ordered to detrack. Proponents of the idea of providing all students with an academically rigorous curriculum viewed detracking as a step toward equality of opportunity to learn and a way to create socially just schools. It was expected that detracking efforts would involve technical challenges, such as changes in scheduling and organization of classes, but these proved not to be the only or even the major obstacles to detracking. In their study, Oakes and Wells (1996; Wells & Oakes, 1996) found that schools that tried to implement detracking encountered powerful normative and political obstacles. One obstacle to detracking was the traditional conceptualization of intelligence as innate and fixed. Many educators and parents viewed intelligence as a genetic characteristic that could not be influenced by school. Additionally, opponents of detracking believed that most students were not capable of a rigorous curriculum, and detracking would be "dumbing down" or "watering down" the curriculum. This, they argued, would be particularly unfair to "naturally" high-ability students who would be held back from their full academic potential. In addition, opposition was fueled by the idea that Latinos, African Americans, and low SES students were not "naturally" intelligent or of high ability and thus could not handle, let alone deserve, a rigorous curriculum.

Another barrier to detracking efforts found in these studies was political maneuvering and leveraging by various groups, including politically powerful parents, teachers, and school and district leaders. Because curriculum tracking supports an unequal system in schools linked to power and access to a variety of exclusive and scarce educational resources and opportunities for students in high tracks (e.g., college-bound curriculum, college workshops, experienced and highly qualified teachers), some parents and school officials who served high-track children fought to keep their status and position as their legitimate and exclusive domain and to thwart detracking efforts. They vigorously fought to maintain the status quo of a rigorous curriculum for the select few whom they saw as rightfully deserving of it.

Efforts to detrack schools lost momentum in the 2000s, most likely due to increased emphasis on standardized testing and accountability. A return to detracking efforts could have a large impact on Mexican American students since they are largely underrepresented in high tracks. Detracking would provide Mexican American students (as well as other underrepresented groups) access to high-status knowledge and skills, a challenging curriculum, college preparatory courses, and opportunities to develop cross-racial relationships.

Concluding Thoughts

This chapter examined various conditions and structures within schools that negatively affect Mexican American academic achievement. Segregation, a phenomenon that many people associate with the history of American schooling, greatly shapes schooling conditions for Mexican Americans today. Many Mexican American students attend segregated schools and, therefore, are more likely to experience inferior educational conditions and poor academic achievement. Additionally, the accountability movement and high-stakes testing within public schools has created additional barriers for their academic success. Overreliance on standardized tests for assessing learning and punitive ways of using them is problematic for Mexican American students. Finally, curriculum tracking, the second generation of segregation (which is often not even recognized as segregation), locks out many Mexican American students from rigorous and challenging curriculum and ensures a low status within schools. Their overrepresentation in low tracks negatively affects academic opportunities in high school and college. Each of these issues, while problematic, can be addressed through new policies that create equitable learning opportunities for Mexican American students.

Discussion Exercises

1. Why has racial segregation in school been increasing for Mexican Americans and other Latinos? Why is this issue of concern?

2. How does concentrated poverty relate to racial segregation in schools? Why would that relationship matter?

3. Identify three key research or policy recommendations to address racial segregation and discuss what concrete actions need to be taken to make them a reality.

4. What have been some of the criticisms against standardized testing and standard-based reforms? Do you consider them valid concerns? Why?

5. Develop a short skit that demonstrates the differences between low and high tracks. How do these differences affect a student's experience at school? Did they affect your educational experiences?

6. Why are Mexican Americans overrepresented in low or non–college bound tracks? How does this overrepresentation affect their educational achievements?

7. What obstacles were encountered in efforts to detrack? How can these be overcome?

Suggested Readings

Oakes, J. (1985). *Keeping track: How schools structure inequality*. New Haven, CT: Yale University Press.

Oakes, J., & Wells, A. S. (1996). *Beyond the technicalities of school reform: Policy lessons from detracking schools*. Los Angeles: UCLA Graduate School of Education and Information Studies.

Ochoa, G. (2013). *Academic profiling: Latinos, Asian Americans, and the achievement gap*. Minneapolis: University of Minnesota Press.

Orfield, G. (2001). *Schools more separate: Consequences of a decade of resegregation*. Cambridge, MA: The Civil Rights Project at Harvard University.

Orfield, G., & Kornhaber, M. L. (2001). *Raising standards or raising barriers? Inequality and high-stakes testing in public education*. New York: Century Foundation Press.

Valenzuela, A. (2005). *Leaving children behind: How "Texas-style" accountability fails Latino youth*. Albany: State University of New York Press.

Chapter 3

The Politics of Spanish and Bilingualism

What language or languages do you speak? On the surface, language would seem to be a benign and noncontroversial issue. At best, one that might elicit pride if one knows more than one language or at worst, embarrassment for stumbling over the words of a newly acquired language. However, language has often been at the center of many contentious battles in the United States. These battles are rooted in our society's ongoing ideological struggle over what it means to be an American and what kind of country America should be. Mexican-origin people have been a part of these language battles since the United States annexed a large part of Mexico in 1848. Nevertheless, the Spanish language and Mexican culture have been considered foreign and, therefore, have been viewed as phenomenon not really American. Unlike most immigrant groups, Mexican immigration is set apart due to the proximity of the countries that includes a large shared border and a Mexican immigration flow that has surged and slowed over time but never completely stopped. As a result of this immigration history and recent increases in the immigration of Mexican and other Spanish-speaking Latino groups, conflict over the use of Spanish and integration of Mexican culture in American society have become a part of public and political debate and policy. These debates and policies have affected the educational system directly through the methods in which schools educate linguistic-minority students who are predominantly Mexican American and Spanish speakers. This chapter examines how non-English languages have been viewed in the United States, educational issues for linguistic-minority and English learner students, and the debate over bilingual education.

The Contentiousness of Language

Language has long been a touchy topic in American society. A nation built by diverse native and immigrant peoples from around the world has struggled with how to incorporate them and become a unified nation. Learning English and not maintaining non-English native languages has been considered central to this mission. Without this, many political leaders believed the balkanization of various racial/ethnic groups into their own enclaves—each retaining their native language and culture—would lead to the demise of America. There would be social, political, and economic dissonance and disintegration. Are non-English languages and cultures a threat to American unity? Should there only be one language (English) and one American culture in the nation? Mexican Americans have been a part of these debates that have characterized Spanish and Mexican culture as threatening and, more recently, potentially engulfing. The conceptualization of the "Latinoization" or "Hispanization" of the United States as a threat has often been an important component of public and school policy changes regarding immigrants and language.

In academia, assimilation theory was developed to understand the process of how a diverse American society could homogenize linguistically, culturally, and in other ways (see Gordon, 1964; Park, 1950; Park & Burgess, 1924). It was believed that theoretically America would and should become a "melting pot" society as a result of the merging of immigrant groups. That is, immigrants would come to America and assimilate or "melt" into the larger society. Assimilation was thought to be the natural process of shedding native cultures and languages by immigrants and adopting the English language and American values and way of life. Assimilation would take place in various stages that included language and cultural changes, residential integration, structural assimilation (where immigrant groups become similar in education, income, and occupation to the majority), and marital assimilation through intergroup marriage (referred to as **amalgamation**) (Gordon, 1964). Based largely on eastern and southern European immigrant groups, assimilation was assumed to be the path for racial/ethnic groups that followed. In reality, the history of the United States documents the social norms, covenants, and laws that prohibited social and residential integration and antimiscegenation laws that outlawed intermarriage. As discussed in chapter 1, segregationist norms and policies affected Mexican Americans in schools but also were a part of social, labor market, and residential life.

Given the history of segregation, assimilation has not been a straight path in all areas for Mexican Americans, most notably structural assimilation. Many scholars have argued that Mexican American assimilation has been impeded by a history of **racialization**, which has relegated them to the bottom of the American social hierarchy (Acuña, 1972; Barrera, 1979; Telles & Ortiz, 2008). Telles and Ortiz's research shows that, in particular, low levels of education have limited socioeconomic assimilation and continue to keep the third generation (grandchildren of immigrants) and beyond in a low social status. Additionally, in terms of language assimilation, Mexican Americans resemble many prior immigrant groups (albeit slower) so that by the third and fourth generations, most are **monolingual** English speakers and do not speak Spanish. Nevertheless, the question of assimilation for Mexican Americans is constantly at the forefront when language and cultural battles emerge due to Mexico's proximity and mostly continuous Mexican immigration. This immigration revitalizes Spanish-speaking communities and reintegrates Spanish and aspects of Mexican culture into them and into mainstream venues (e.g., Spanglish radio stations, cable TV stations and packages specifically for Spanish speakers).

While the desire for some level of assimilation has been partly fueled by the goal of a unified country, it has also been fueled by **xenophobia**, a feared loss of political and economic power, and ideologies of racial superiority (Gonzalez, 1990, 2000; Menchaca, 1995, 1997; Spring, 2011). Fear of the impact of non-Anglo Protestant culture and non-English languages, including Spanish and Mexican culture, on American society created anxieties about societal polarization and decline. In addition, America as a melting pot would also preserve the existing political and economic interests and keep power in the hands of elite Anglo Protestants. Finally, support of assimilation was also partially motivated by the idea that not all races and cultures are equal. Despite the term *melting pot*, the ideology was not really about merging various cultures to form a new American culture but about changing "foreign" cultures to what was considered a real American language (English) and culture (Anglo Protestant) (Spring, 2011). Therefore, even now, the idea of a continued Spanish language and Mexican cultural presence in the United States is oftentimes considered problematic to those who advocate the idea of a single and exclusive American language and unchanging and narrow cultural ideal.

This debate about language did not begin with Mexican-origin people or even with the establishment of the United States. Even before the official formation of the United States, there was a level of fear both by politicians and the public of what might happen if non–English speaking and non-Anglo immigrant groups did not change their native cultures and language.

Consequently, the idea of using the educational system to promote the English language and Anglo American values began early. Historian Lawrence Cremin (1970) notes that William Smith, an educator and school administrator, proclaimed in 1753, "By a common education of English and German youth at the same schools, acquaintances and connections will be formed, and deeply impressed upon them in their cheerful and open moments. The English language and a conformity of manners will be acquired" (as cited in Spring, 2011, p. 24). Based on a similar mind-set of assimilating German youth in the eighteenth century, Benjamin Franklin proposed the establishment of English-language schools in order to halt the spread of German and to promote Anglicization (Spring, 2011). Thus, schools became the location where intentionally assimilative practices were established.

Using schools in an attempt to shape and unify students from diverse backgrounds became more formalized with the creation of common schools (public schools) in the 1830s. Though some groups were too poor to attend school, excluded from school, or sent to segregated schools, this was the first attempt to standardize the schooling experience with the goal of shaping a future society unified in language and moral and political beliefs. As discussed in chapter 1, for Mexican Americans, this began in the nineteenth century with the exclusion of Spanish and Mexican history from schools. In the early twentieth century, Americanization programs were one response to perceived threats of the Spanish language and Mexican culture. Americanization programs were an important part of these standardizing efforts, and deculturalization was a critical component of them. Mexican American students were prohibited from and punished for speaking Spanish in school. They were also taught a curriculum designed to instill an Anglo American value system and way of life. A monolingual and monocultural citizenry were the desired outcomes of Americanization policies. The policies were also motivated by the perceived inferiority of the Spanish language and Mexican culture. Therefore, the intent of the policies was to replace an inferior language and culture with purportedly superior ones—English and Anglo American culture (Gonzalez, 1990; Spring, 2011).

Debunking the Myths: Immigrants and Their Children Learn English

Prevalent myths about non–English speaking immigrants serve to fuel hostility toward them and their native languages. Some popular myths are that immigrants resist learning English, cling to their native languages, segregate themselves by language from mainstream society, and perpetuate their native language to later generations (Tse, 2001). These beliefs are commonly held by the general public and are often revealed in popular press opinion pieces lamenting the lack of immigrant willingness to learn English and by politicians seeking to create language policies that focus on English acquisition. However, these myths about immigrants are unfounded, and recent data on Latinos substantiate this.

Data from the Pew Hispanic Center show that an overwhelming majority of Latinos believe learning English is important and want future U.S. Latinos to speak English. Similar to that of previous immigrants, Latinos' acquisition of English is more pronounced, with each successive generation in the United States: 38 percent, 92 percent, and 96 percent of the first, second, and third generation, respectively, report speaking English "very well" or "pretty well" (Taylor, Lopez, Martinez, & Velasco, 2012). Despite evidence contradicting the myths about immigrants resisting English and clinging to native languages, these beliefs continue to underlie public and political debates and fuel hostility.

In recent decades, the ongoing ideological and political battles about language and culture have intensified with increased immigration to the United States. The growth of Mexican American and Latino communities has led to increased visibility of these communities and use of Spanish in public spaces (e.g., billboards, intercom announcements in grocery stores). Therefore, political backlashes have been particularly focused on Mexican and Latino immigration and the Spanish language. With the burgeoning population of Mexican American and Latino students, part of the backlash has been targeted at schools and affected the treatment of linguistic minorities and English learners (ELs).

Linguistic Minorities and English Learners

A pressing issue in American education today especially relevant to Mexican American students is serving the needs of increasing numbers of linguistic minorities and English learners. The linguistic-minority population of school-aged children in the United States has increased by 130 percent from 1980 to 2005 (Rumberger, 2006). Table 6 shows data about linguistic-minority children whose home language is Spanish and who are of Mexican origin.

Table 6. Children Ages Five to Seventeen Who Spoke a Language Other than English at Home, by Selected Characteristics, 2009

	TOTAL POPULATION, AGES FIVE TO SEVENTEEN (IN MILLIONS)	SPOKE A LANGUAGE OTHER THAN ENGLISH AT HOME	
		Number (in Millions)	Percentage
Total	53.3	11.2	21.0
Spanish Home Language	8.0	8.0	100.0
Mexican-Origin	7.9	5.3	68.0

Source: Aud et al., 2011, table A-6-2

These National Center for Education Statistics data show that there are about 11.2 million public school children in the United States whose home language is not English. This represents about one in five school-age children. Spanish is the predominant home language spoken among linguistic minorities; about 71 percent of linguistic-minority students come from Spanish-speaking homes (8 of 11.2 million). Mexican Americans make up about 5 million or almost 50 percent of all linguistic-minority students in the United States. Table 6 also shows that among the Mexican American school-age population, about 68 percent are linguistic minorities (Aud et al., 2011). Therefore, Mexican American students are largely linguistic minorities and comprise almost one in two linguistic-minority students nationally.

Linguistic minorities may begin school with a range of proficiency in English. Those needing to acquire English proficiency are designated as English learners. There are about 4.7 million English learners in U.S. public schools, making up about one in ten students (Aud et al., 2012), the majority of whom are U.S.-born citizens. Four states have more than 14 percent ELs in their public school population: Texas, New Mexico, Nevada, and California. The states with the largest actual numbers of ELs are California, Texas, Florida, New York, and Illinois (Aud et al., 2012). States in the South such as Georgia, Alabama, Arkansas, and Tennessee, however, are now experiencing the most rapid growth of ELs (Gándara & Hopkins, 2010).

Achievement Gap for English Learners

A central issue in the education of English learners is the gap on various measures of educational outcomes in comparison to English-proficient students. ELs are about twice as likely to be pushed out of school as fluent English speakers and former ELs (Callahan, 2013), and nearly half of states graduate less than 60 percent of ELs (Stetser & Stillwell, 2014). Additionally, research shows that the standardized test scores of ELs are considerably lower than the achievement of native English speakers (Fry, 2007; Gándara & Rumberger, 2002; Mahon, 2006)

Scholars have noted that one important issue in the achievement gap of English learners is their assessment in a language in which they are not proficient (Gándara & Rumberger, 2002). In addition, most standardized tests are not developed with English learners in mind and, thus, are not appropriate assessments for them (R. W. Solórzano, 2008; Valdés & Figueroa, 1994). This context contributes to achievement gaps between English learners and English-only students. Nevertheless, English learners are often evaluated with district, state, and national assessments in English and, oftentimes, bear the same consequences of these assessments as English-only students.

Based on National Assessment of Educational Progress (NAEP), a gap in reading and math test scores is evident between English learners and non–English learners. Figure 8 shows a persistent discrepancy in reading scores throughout fourth, eighth, and twelfth grades. Likewise, figure 9 shows a gap in math scores throughout primary and secondary school grades.

NAEP data (not shown in figures) also show that in eighth grade 69 percent and 70 percent of ELs are "below basic" in math and reading, respectively, in comparison to 24 percent and 20 percent of non-ELs (National Center for Education Statistics, 2014). These gaps in achievement are

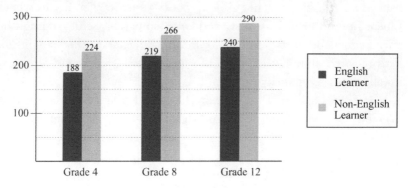

Figure 8. Average reading scores, by grade and English proficiency, 2009. Source: Aud et al. (2012).

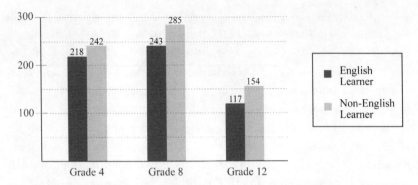

Figure 9. Average math scores, by grade and English proficiency, 2009. Source: Aud et al. (2012).

increasingly important given the current era of punitive repercussions of low test scores for students and schools. Moreover, they are important for preparation for college and future career skills.

These gaps in achievement have been shown to persist throughout elementary and secondary schooling and even for students who are reclassified as proficient in English. Based on research in California, where almost 30 percent of all linguistic-minority students live, and about 85 percent of English learners are Spanish speaking, Gándara and Rumberger (2002) found that English learners (both ELs and Reclassified Fluent English Proficient [R-FEP]) consistently lag behind English-only students on reading achievement from grades two through eleven. The discrepancy in scores was highlighted by the finding that in eleventh grade EL and R-FEP students reach the reading scores that English-only students achieve in the middle of sixth grade—a gap of about four and a half years. Additionally, linguistic-minority students who began school Fluent English Proficient (FEP) and with comparable scores to English-only students began falling behind in third grade and never caught up. This research illuminates the need for proper assessments and resources for all linguistic-minority students.

Many states have high school exit exams, and recent data suggest that overall ELs are not doing as well as English-only students. English learners are at a disadvantage because high school exit exams measure both subject content and English language ability. In states with exit exams where the majority of Mexican American students live, the pass rates vary widely but nonetheless consistently show a gap with the state's overall student population. Passage rates for ELs by the end of twelfth grade were 76 percent in California and 20.2 percent in Arizona, in comparison to 91 percent and 71 percent, respectively, for the overall student population. In Texas, a state with the longest history of exit exams, pass rates for ELs were about 50 percent in both English language arts and math, in comparison to 94 percent and 84 percent, respectively, for the overall student population (Center on Education Policy, 2007). Unfortunately, even former EL students lag behind on exit exam pass rates. California Department of Education data show that 62 percent of English learners and former EL tenth-grade students passed the exit exam as compared to 83 percent of Initial Fluent English Proficient (I-FEP) and English-only students (Gándara & Rumberger, 2006). Results such as these exemplify why there is concern for ELs on achievement tests and on high-stakes tests that are gatekeepers to educational mobility.

Unequal School Conditions for English Learners

While English learners may need additional educational resources that native English speakers do not, they instead receive unequal and inferior resources in many areas. Figure 10 summarizes seven factors that Gándara, Rumberger, Maxwell-Jolly, and Callahan (2003) have identified

1.	Inequitable access to appropriately trained teachers
2.	Inadequate professional development opportunities to help teachers address the instructional needs of English learners
3.	Inequitable access to appropriate assessment to measure EL achievement, gauge their learning needs, and hold the system accountable for their progress
4.	Inadequate instructional time to accomplish learning goals
5.	Inequitable access to instructional materials and curriculum
6.	Inequitable access to adequate facilities
7.	Intense segregation into schools and classrooms that place them at particularly high risk for educational failure

Figure 10. Unequal educational conditions for English learners. Source: Gándara, Rumberger, Maxwell-Jolly, and Callahan (2003).

as contributing to unequal schooling conditions and possibly contributing to achievement gaps for English learners.

This study found that ELs were more likely than other children to be taught by teachers with emergency credentials and that almost one-quarter of teachers of ELs in California were not fully credentialed. Teachers of EL students also did not have enough or had low-quality professional training to meet the needs of that student population. Additionally, ELs did not have sufficient instructional time because they participate in pull-out programs or other English learner classes, which takes time away from learning other academic subjects. Teachers of ELs also report not having enough access to textbooks and other instructional materials.

Many English learners face a double challenge in school: they need to learn English, and they are overwhelmingly poor. Research has shown that at least 80 percent of English learners are economically disadvantaged. They are also likely to be concentrated in schools where the majority of students are also poor and English learners (Baker & Hakuta, 1997; Gándara, Maxwell-Jolly, & Rumberger, 2008). Thus, they face socioeconomic and linguistic segregation in school. These characteristics contribute to a disadvantaged learning environment for English learners because of constrained school and community resources and limited exposure to English language models.

Recommendations for English Learners

To address the unequal learning conditions identified above, the following need to be realized for English learners (for specific policies, see Gándara, Maxwell-Jolly, and Rumberger, 2008):

- Increase access to qualified teachers to address higher likelihood of being taught by student teachers or those with an emergency credential.

- Provide adequate materials and good schooling conditions to address less access to linguistically appropriate textbooks and instructional materials.

- Provide equitable and meaningful assessment for English learners.

- Provide appropriate and rigorous coursework and access to counselors to address lack of such coursework or materials for English learners.

- Provide more instruction time to address being pulled out of regular classes, having multiple periods of English as a Second Language classes, and having fewer teaching assistants to provide individualized time.

- Increase professional development for teachers of English learners.

- Address effects of segregation of English learners due to isolation in socioeconomically and linguistically segregated schools.

Learning Academic English

Despite popular notions, learning English is not a task that happens quickly—even for children. Research has shown that English learners require from five to seven years to attain English proficiency. Moreover, there is a difference in the time needed to attain oral proficiency and proficiency in writing and reading. One study found that oral proficiency may be acquired in about three to five years while proficiency in writing and reading requires about four to seven years (Hakuta, Butler, & Witt, 2000). Other studies have documented a similar time frame of six to ten years to attain English proficiency. Of utmost importance, however, is that English learners acquire *academic English*, which is different from basic speaking and comprehension skills. Academic English is the level of English necessary for academic success in high school and especially college. Academic English requires mastery of an extensive range of English (e.g., word forms and grammar) and of specific linguistic functions such as persuading, arguing, and hypothesizing (U.C. Language Minority Research Institute, 2000). Thus, while one might assume that basic speaking and comprehension of English (conversational or interpersonal conversation) is all that is necessary for mainstreaming English learners to English-only classes, it is not the oral, written, or reading level needed to adequately support academic success. Unfortunately, even most bilingual education programs in the United States have not been modeled to meet this standard.

Bilingual Education Policies and Court Decisions

While linguistic-minority students in public schools speak many different languages, because an overwhelming proportion of English learner students are Spanish speakers, bilingual education has been considered largely a Latino issue (Baker & Hakuta, 1997). Moreover, Mexican-origin students are a sizable proportion of those Spanish speakers and, thus, have been affected greatly by bilingual education policies and court cases. Beginning in the 1960s, the federal government and courts established several pieces of legislation that addressed the educational rights of linguistic-minority students. The intent of those policies, however, was not always clearly articulated. Speaking about the first major bilingual education legislation, the Bilingual Education Act (BEA) of 1968, English learner advocate James Crawford (2000) dissects the lack of clarity:

> Was this 1968 law intended primarily to assimilate limited-English-proficient (LEP) children more efficiently, to teach them English as rapidly as possible, to encourage bilingualism and biliteracy, to remedy academic underachievement and high dropout rates, to raise the self-esteem of minority students, to promote social equality, or to pursue all of these goals simultaneously? (p. 107)

As with other aspects of bilingual education, the intention of this policy was ambiguous, and therefore implementation in schools varied. Additionally, various scholars have noted that bilingual education policies were based on a deficit perspective. That is, policies were directed at fixing so-called deficiencies of linguistic minorities—namely not speaking English. Moreover, the native languages of ELs were not viewed as a resource to be cultivated but as a barrier to be overcome (García & Wiese, 2002).

Several major policies and court decisions were instrumental in the development of bilingual education that affected Mexican American students. These emerged at the height of civil rights advocacy and a societal focus on addressing issues affecting poor people and people of color, including linguistic minorities. The previously mentioned BEA of 1968, or Title VII of the Elementary and Secondary Education Act, was the first federal policy aimed at addressing the unique educational needs of English learners (called limited English proficient). The goal of this policy was to create educational programs for EL students to provide them with equal access to the curriculum. However, it was not intended to shape a language policy and did not specify types of programs or instructional methods for schools.

In *Lau v. Nichols* (1974), the Supreme Court ruled that schools had to provide an education that was understandable to students with limited proficiency in English. *Lau* was a class action suit filed on behalf of 1,800 Chinese-ancestry students in San Francisco who were not fluent in English and not receiving supplemental courses in the English language. The suit argued that these students were not provided with adequate instructional programs and, therefore, were denied equal educational opportunities. The Court ruled that limited English proficient children must be able to effectively participate in educational programs and must be provided special instructional programs to meet their learning needs. As with the BEA, no specific instructional approach was urged; however, schools needed to take affirmative steps to rectify "language deficiencies."

The 1974 reauthorization of the BEA of 1968 established a link between equal opportunity and bilingual education programs and defined bilingual education to include native language instruction. Bilingual education was defined as "instruction given in, and study of, English, and, to the extent necessary to allow a child to progress effectively through the educational system, the native language" (sec, 703 [a][4][A][i] as cited in García & Wiese, 2002). However, in 1984, an important change in the policy occurred; the reauthorization of the BEA shifted from mandating only bilingual programs to accepting English-only programs as well, with funding preferred for the latter programs. These latter programs were called transitional bilingual education programs and emphasized structured instruction in English and native language instruction, only as necessary, to support English language instruction. A second type of program, developmental bilingual, was to provide structured English instruction and native language instruction so as to achieve competence in both.

In addition to these major pieces of legislation, several lawsuits were brought about by Latino litigants regarding the education of English learners, including lawsuits refining prior legislation. As a result, *Aspira of New York, Inc. v. Board of Education* (1975) established a procedure for identifying Spanish-dominant children so that they could be placed into a Spanish language program. Another lawsuit, *Castañeda v. Pickard* (1981), narrowed the "appropriate action" to be taken by schools to provide adequate instructional programs to meet the learning needs of English learners. Although the court did not specify an instruction program, it did specify that an educational program for linguistic-minority children must follow three standards: (1) it must be based on a sound educational theory; (2) it must be implemented effectively with sufficient qualified staff; and (3) after a trial period, it must be evaluated as effective in overcoming language barriers (García & Wiese, 2002).

Bilingual Education Programs

Even before recent efforts to do away with bilingual education (discussion forthcoming), all English learners have not had access to bilingual education, and there has been great variation in the types of instructional programs they have been provided (see García & Baker, 2007, and Ovando, Combs, & Collier, 2006, for overviews). Macias (1997) in a study for the Office of Bilingual Education and Minority Languages Affairs found that only 30 percent of ELs were in programs that had academic instruction in their native language, and an additional 22 percent had "informal" support in their native language (as cited in Krashen, 1999). Therefore, most English learners were not in any form of bilingual education. Even those in some form of bilingual education had varied amounts of native language and English instructional time. Hopstock et al., (1993) in a study for the U.S. Department of Education, found that of those in some kind of bilingual program, about one-third were taught more than 75 percent of the time in English, another third were taught 40 percent to 75 percent of the time in English, and the final third less than 40 percent of the time in English (as cited in Crawford, 2008).

The most common form of bilingual education in the United States has been the transitional (or early exit) bilingual program. Typically, transitional bilingual education provides English learners with one to three years of native language and sheltered English instruction in subject areas as well as English as a second language (ESL) instruction. A goal of transitional bilingual programs is to mainstream ELs to English-only as quickly as possible. The number of years in transitional bilingual programs does not reflect the number of years necessary to acquire academic English, and, therefore, some scholars argue that ELs in this type of program are typically mainstreamed too early. A second type of bilingual education is called developmental (also called maintenance or late-exit). This model usually provides native language and sheltered English instruction in subject areas and ESL instruction. The duration of this program is from five to seven years, or the time typically needed to acquire academic English.

A third type of bilingual education is dual-language immersion (or two-way immersion). Typically, this type of model attempts to balance ELs with English speakers in an integrated classroom. Subject area knowledge is taught in both the native language and English. Two models of dual-language programs are 50–50 and 90–10. The 50–50 model divides use of the native language and English equally throughout all grade levels. The 90–10 model begins in kindergarten using 90 percent native language and 10 percent English language instruction and gradually increases the percentage of English instruction as the grade level increases (e.g., 80–20 in first grade, 70–30 in second) so that by the upper elementary grades instruction is divided 50–50 by language.

In addition to these types of bilingual education models, schools that serve ELs may have support programs such as English as a second language (ESL) or English for speakers of other languages (ESOL). These are often pullout programs (which may require ELs to leave English-only classes for instruction in another class) and may vary in emphasis on the development of English language grammar skills or verbal usage. There are also ESL content classes that teach academic content with specific instructional methods for ELs. Thomas and Collier (1997) found that ESL pullout programs are the most common and, unfortunately, the least effective (as cited in Ovando et al., 2006) because students miss the full curriculum (due to being pulled out) and do not have access to native language instruction to assist them with academic work while they learn English. Studies (e.g., Ramirez, Yuen, Ramey & Pasta, 1991; Thomas & Collier, 1997) have found that English learners do better academically in developmental bilingual education and dual-language immersion programs than in transitional bilingual education and do better in transitional bilingual education than ESL pullout programs (as cited in Ovando et al., 2006).

There is often confusion about these programs because the same term is used to label programs that may have different goals and student populations. A major ideological distinction exists between transitional bilingual education and dual-language (or two-way) programs. As previously mentioned, the main goal of transitional programs is English language development and mainstreaming students to English-only classes as quickly as possible. This type of program has been referred to as **subtractive bilingualism** due to the goal of *replacing* students' native language with English. Learning English is the overarching emphasis, and there is no attempt to maintain the native language or place any value on speaking, writing, and reading it. In contrast, the goal of dual-language programs is bilingualism, biliteracy, and academic achievement in two languages. This type of program has been referred to as additive bilingualism because English is developed along with the development of the native language (Freeman, 2004).

Bilingual Education or English Only

Research has shown that bilingual education is an effective instructional method for English learners (Cummins, 1989; Krashen, 1996; Willig, 1985). In fact, research has shown that children in well-structured bilingual programs consistently do better than students in English-only programs or at least have some advantage over English-only programs. For example, a major federal study found that developmental bilingual education was best for promoting academic achievement in English and bilingualism (Ramirez et al., 1991). Many scholars agree that bilingual education promotes subject matter knowledge and literacy. That is, students are able to keep pace learning new material in their native language, while not falling progressively behind, and develop literacy in their first language, which facilitates literacy in English. Language skills developed in a native language do transfer to English and make learning it easier (Krashen, 1999). In addition, research on bilingual children has shown that they have some advantages over monolingual children. Bilingualism has positive effects in many areas, including cognitive performance measures, metalinguistic qualities, divergent thinking, and creativity (Soto, 1997).

If bilingual education is effective for ELs, then why has it not been supported and instead dismantled in the last decades? Advocates of bilingual education argue that recent efforts to end bilingual education may be partly motivated by a variety of factors, including fear of Spanish and the Latinoization of the country, fear of a loss of power, a desire to keep a monolithic ideology and culture in the United States, and lack of knowledge by the general public on the benefits of bilingual education.

Dismantling Bilingual Education: English-Only and Anti–Bilingual Education Initiatives

What is best for English learners in school is not only influenced by educators and parents but oftentimes by public mood and politicians. In the late 1960s, federal initiatives acknowledged the special instructional needs of English learners and, therefore, formally ushered in bilingual education. In the past few decades, however, public mood and political interventions have played a role in creating policies severely restricting access to bilingual education. The English-only movement and several state and federal initiatives have been influential in limiting access to native language instruction for ELs. Since Spanish-speaking Mexican Americans and other

Latino students represent the largest group to receive bilingual education and other services for ELs, they are most affected by these changes.

ENGLISH ONLY. Beginning in the 1980s, the English-only movement began as public sentiment seemed to turn against bilingual education and immigrants. In that decade, the organizations English First and U.S. English were founded to advocate for English as the nation's official language and to advocate against bilingual policies and programs. While unsuccessful on a national level in making English the official language, many states did follow the impetus with measures to make English the official state language, beginning a rally against bilingual education. U.S. English founder Senator S. I. Hayakawa of California argued that the impact of bilingual programs "was to maintain Spanish language enclaves, discourage immigrants from assimilating, and encourage Quebec-style separatism" (as cited in Crawford, 2008, p. 84). U.S. English presented bilingual education as intentionally clannish and divisive.

The English-only movement claimed that contemporary immigrants, especially Mexican-origin and other Latinos, were different from previous generations of immigrants. English First claimed immigrants were unwilling to learn English and an economic burden to the American taxpayer. One English First (1986) publication stated,

> Tragically, many immigrants these days refuse to learn English! They never become productive members of society. They remain stuck in a linguistic and economic ghetto, many living off welfare and costing working Americans millions of tax dollars every year. (as cited in Crawford, 2008, p. 18)

Contemporary immigrants and bilingual education were portrayed as divisive, anti-American, and anti-English. While fear of immigrants and non-English languages is not new, U.S. English and English First initiated the anti-immigrant and English-only rhetoric and legal actions in the 1980s that continued into the following decades.

ANTI–BILINGUAL EDUCATION STATE INITIATIVES. In 1998, Californians voted overwhelmingly in support of anti–bilingual education initiative Proposition 227 (61 percent in favor). The initiative mandated that all non–English speaking children be taught in English and prohibited the use of or development of native languages for non–English speaking students in school. The initiative effectively called for the end of bilingual education.

Similar anti–bilingual education initiatives were passed or proposed to ban native language instruction in several other states. In 2000, Arizona passed Proposition 203, which also sought to eliminate bilingual education. As with Proposition 227, one year of intensive English instruction was the prescribed educational plan for ELs before mainstreaming them into English-only classrooms. In 2002, two additional anti–bilingual education initiatives were put forth in Massachusetts and Colorado. The Massachusetts English in Public Schools Initiative (also known as Question 2) passed overwhelmingly by 61 percent of voters. In Colorado, the antibilingual initiative, Amendment 31, was defeated (56 percent to 44 percent). In 2008, a similar English-only initiative (Measure 58) was also defeated in Oregon.

NO CHILD LEFT BEHIND. As discussed in chapter 2, in 2002, the federal government reauthorized the Elementary and Secondary Education Act of 1965 as the renamed No Child Left Behind (NCLB). NCLB created a system of high-stakes testing for public school children by mandating state standards and yearly standardized tests. Federal funding to states is dependent on compliance, and though allowing for state variation in standards and content of the tests, every other year a sample of fourth and eighth graders in each state must take the National Assessment of Educational Progress (NAEP) test to compare state test results. All testing is conducted in English, which creates strong incentives for increased emphasis on English-only instruction and decreased emphasis on native languages. Even though NCLB is not a language policy, it has been called a de facto English language policy due to mandates for English language standardized testing and negative repercussions for not meeting yearly goals based on that testing.

English learners (also called limited English proficient, or LEP) are a subgroup monitored separately under NCLB's accountability system. They must be assessed on state assessments for English language proficiency annually. After being in U.S. schools for three years, English learners must be included with all other student populations to make "adequate yearly progress" on target achievement goals in language arts and math, regardless of English proficiency. Critics of NCLB's treatment of English learners argue that this is nearly an impossible task because by definition, ELs are not proficient in reading and math due to language barriers. Finally, the standardized tests mandated by NCLB were designed for English speakers and therefore, there is no way of knowing if they are valid and reliable for assessing English learners. Nevertheless, NCLB mandates that all students, including English learners, be "proficient" by 2014, and schools not meeting this goal would suffer staff reassignment, school takeover, or school closure. Since NCLB's inception, no state has ever achieved 100 percent proficiency. Thus, the majority of states currently have waivers or extensions on waivers that exempt them from this unattainable goal.

NCLB had a detrimental effect on bilingual education. Taking the position that bilingual education has not been beneficial for ELs, NCLB sought to bring an end to bilingual education. NCLB repealed the Bilingual Education Act, and, in keeping with this move, the Office of Bilingual Education and Minority Languages Affairs was renamed the Office of English Language Acquisition, Language Enhancement, and Academic Achievement for Limited-English-Proficient Students. While funds are still allocated to the instructional needs of ELs, the funds are focused on the goal of learning English as quickly as possible through the use of English-only immersion programs.

Multiculturalism and Bilingualism as a Plus

The view of English learners as problematic in American public schools has influenced their treatment. While additional languages may be required in high school for graduation and college admission and seen as a potential benefit for the job market, children who come to school speaking a native language other than English have not been viewed as having a valued resource. Instead, they have been viewed as disadvantaged. The singular focus has been on English acquisition, while the native language is neglected, made irrelevant, and eventually forgotten. The extraction of the cultural and linguistic capital that Mexican American students bring to school has been called "subtractive schooling" and involves the process of "de-Mexicanization" (Gándara, 1999a). However, many multicultural and bilingual advocates argue that English learners and students of color have resources—their native language and culture—that could facilitate learning, enrich the learning environment, and benefit the child and society. They argue that these resources should be welcomed and cultivated in school and are essential to learning.

English Plus, a campaign launched in response to the English-only movement, argues that while English is the dominant language and necessary to learn in the United States, knowing or learning two or more languages is in the best interest of the United States. The organization's philosophy as articulated in their statement of purpose is that

> by promoting cultural and democratic pluralism within our own borders, we also enhance our economic competitiveness and maintain our international leadership. In an interdependent world, the diversity of our people provides a unique reservoir of abilities and resources. The English Plus concept holds that the national interest is best served when all members of our society have full access to effective opportunities to acquire strong English language proficiency plus mastery of a second or multiple languages. ("English Plus movement: Statement of purpose & core beliefs," 1987)

Crawford (2008) summarizes key reasons beyond national interests as to why maintaining native languages is beneficial (see figure 11). First, research has shown that being proficient in two languages is correlated with greater mental flexibility. Studies have shown that English learners who develop language skills in their native language have academic advantages in the long run. Second, learning a native language can help with ethnic ambivalence and alienation. Youth can explore and be proud of their heritage. Third, bilingualism can help with family communication in immigrant families. Children can feel distant from their parents and grandparents if they are not proficient in their native language. Bilingual children are often closer to their parents and can help them as "language brokers" in situations where English proficiency is necessary. Fourth, bilingualism and biliteracy are increasingly valued by employers due to the needs of our diverse society and for conducting business in a global market.

1. cognitive and academic growth

2. help with identity conflicts

3. promotes family values

4. career advantages

5. cultural vitality

Figure 11. Summary benefits of bilingualism.

Finally, maintaining native languages permits access to the arts and ways of life that form a core of cultural vitality (see Cummins, 1979; Hakuta, 1986; Hakuta et al., 2000; Krashen, Tse, & McQuillan, 1998; Ramirez et al., 1991; Tse, 2001; Wong Filmore, 1991).

Advocates of multicultural and bilingual education argue that cultivating native languages and cultures is also about empowerment and cultural democracy (more on multiculturalism in chapter 5). Liberatory models of multicultural and bilingual education value and integrate the languages, histories, and cultures of students of color and consider them to have a rightful place in school and American society. Students' background and life experiences are not incidental or marginal to learning in school but are essential (Maceda, 1997; Valenzuela, 1999).

Gándara, Hopkins, and Martinez (2011) propose taking an "assets view" of language and culture for Latino students. This perspective recognizes the value of and need to build on Latino students' language and cultural knowledge to promote academic success. They propose the following steps for educators and policymakers:

- Actively support federal and state legislation that encourages the use of bilingual instruction.
- Develop multicultural dual-language programs for students across the K–12 continuum.
- Provide rich professional development for all teachers that builds on Latino students' cultural and linguistic assets.
- Promote the development of bilingual educators by offering incentives.
- Secure college counseling positions at schools with high Latino populations and train counselors to use the skills and resources of Latino students and families. (Asserting an Assets View section, para. 11)

Later-Generation Mexican Americans

While this chapter has overwhelmingly focused on linguistic minorities who speak Spanish or live in a home where it is spoken, an important group not spotlighted in discussions on language is later-generation Mexican Americans (LGMA). These are Mexican Americans who are the third generation or more to live in the United States. As discussed previously, by the third generation, Mexican Americans are predominantly English monolingual. Yet research has shown that later-generation Mexican Americans tend to stagnate in both educational and occupational mobility. In fact, some research has shown a decline in educational attainment for LGMA as compared to second-generation Mexican Americans. Therefore, a lack of education has secured their position in the working class (Chávez, 2007; Ortiz, 1996; Telles & Ortiz, 2008).

LGMA are both largely English monolingual and orientated to American culture but have not experienced the academic mobility to be expected for groups with those attributes. Moreover, LGMA have the advantages of citizenship and familiarity with the American educational system (Chávez-Reyes, 2010). Chávez-Reyes (2010) explains this contradiction as a result of racialization and social class status. Although different from immigrant and second-generation Mexican American students, LGMA are indistinguishable to school personnel. As a result, they may experience racial bias through neglect or lack of guidance for academics and career. Additionally, as largely working-class students, LGMA face the expectation that they are not "college material" and are tracked into general or vocational programs and not provided the needed guidance to prepare for college. Due to the lack of educational capital by working-class parents in schools, intervention by school counselors is essential, Chávez-Reyes advocates, for LGMA to access information about college preparation and career opportunities.

Another issue for some later-generation Mexican Americans is the use of Mexican American or Chicano English (varieties include Spanglish, Pachuco, Caló, and TexMex). These multidimensional and fluid dialects have persisted for generations yet are considered by some school officials and educators to be simply deficient and inferior nonstandard forms of English. LGMA who speak Chicano English dialects may be perceived as unintelligent or having a disadvantage that needs "fixing" from the perspective of school personnel. On the contrary, Delpit (1995) argues that the linguistic skills students come to school with are valuable and essential to their learning. She states that "teachers must acknowledge and validate students' home language without using it to limit students' potential. Students' home discourses are vital to their perception of self and sense of community connectedness" (p. 163). Therefore, recognizing and valuing the linguistic skills of LGMA, who are largely monolingual English speakers but may speak a working-class or Chicano dialect of English, is important to best support their academic needs.

Concluding Thoughts

Language has been a contentious issue in American society that has affected schools. American society's fluctuating unease with linguistic and cultural diversity affects English learners as policies change instructional practices. Today, Mexican American students represent almost one-half of all linguistic minorities and, therefore, are affected greatly by any policy changes regarding English learners. Whereas bilingual education was once considered equal opportunity for English learners, the tide has turned, and for antibilingual education advocates, English immersion is being presented as the new equal opportunity. However, bilingual education advocates argue that the current trend toward English-only state initiatives and against bilingual education has created a hostile and subtractive learning environment for Mexican American and other linguistic minorities. While well-structured developmental bilingual programs and dual-language programs have proven effective for the long-term academic achievement of English learners, the emphasis on English-only instruction has gained stronger political footing. Unfortunately, the treatment of English learners in school has not always been guided by what is best for students or by research on the best instructional practices for them but instead by public mood and politics.

Discussion Exercises

1. Why does the author argue that language has been a contentious issue in the United States? Do you agree or disagree with that premise? Why?

2. Why do you think the myths about immigrants discussed in the chapter exist? Can you think of other myths about immigrants? If so, discuss them and their purpose.

3. How might the unequal school conditions for English learners listed in figure 10 affect academic achievement? What other effects might unequal school conditions have?

4. Draw pictures or cartoons illustrating the transitional, developmental, and dual-language bilingual education models. What are the most important differences between models? Why?

5. List four reasons for the English-only movement and antibilingual education state initiatives. Discuss the validity of each reason listed.

6. Discuss the benefits of bilingualism presented in the chapter. Brainstorm a list of other benefits and incorporate them into a poem.

Suggested Readings

Crawford, J. (2008). *Advocating for English learners: Selected essays*. Clevedon, UK: Multilingual Matters.

Gándara, P., & Hopkins, M. (2010). *Forbidden language: English learners and restrictive language policies*. New York: Teachers College Press.

Gándara, P., & Rumberger, R. (2006). *Resource needs for California's English learners*. Los Angeles: UC Linguistic Minority Research Institute.

García, O., & Baker, C. (2007). *Bilingual education: An introductory reader*. Clevedon, UK: Multilingual Matters.

Krashen, S. D. (1999). *Condemned without a trial: Bogus arguments against bilingual education*. Portsmouth, NH: Heinemann.

Tse, L. (2001). *"Why don't they learn English?" Separating fact from fallacy in the U.S. language debate*. New York: Teachers College Press.

Chapter 4

Quest for Higher Education

"Quiero que mi hija vaya a la universidad para que tenga oportunidades que yo nunca tuve." (I want my daughter to go to the university so that she has opportunities that I never had.)

This typical statement by Mexican American parents reflects the desire for higher education for their children to which the majority aspires. In fact, 95 percent of Latino parents say that it is "very" important to them that their children go to college (Pew Hispanic Center and Kaiser Family Foundation, 2004). Moreover, 88 percent of young Latinos say that it is necessary to have a college education to get ahead in life (Pew Hispanic Center, 2009). Even though Latino parents and students overwhelmingly desire higher education, there is a gap between aspirations to go to college and graduation from college. Latinos lag behind other major racial/ethnic groups in graduating with bachelor's, graduate, and professional degrees. Understanding the cause of this gap is critical in order to address its cause and work toward achieving parity.

Despite obstacles on the road to higher education for Mexican Americans, the desire to attend college and the persistence of those who make it show optimism and determination. This chapter illuminates many of the conditions Mexican American students face in pursuit of undergraduate and graduate degrees by discussing their current status and challenges and supports that promote their enrollment and graduation.

Higher Education Portrait

The last thirty years have brought improvement in the enrollment in and completion of college education for Latino students. The number of Latino students enrolled in college increased fivefold from 1976 to 2008 (Aud, Hussar, Planty, Snyder, & Bianco, 2010). In fact, 2012 was the first time that the rate of Latino college enrollment surpassed that of White students among high school graduates (Fry & Taylor, 2013). Additionally, Figure

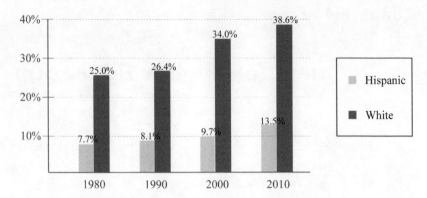

Figure 12. Bachelor's degree or higher among persons twenty-five to twenty-nine years old, by race/ethnicity: 1980–2010. Source: Snyder and Dillon (2011), table 8.

12 shows that the percentage of Latino students aged twenty-five to twenty-nine years who had a bachelor's degree or higher increased from 7.7 percent to 13.5 percent from 1980 to 2010. These are important improvements in higher education over the last decades for Latinos.

As the Mexican American population in the United States continues to grow, more educational changes will take place. Mexican Americans are expected to make up increasing portions of the college-age population within the next decades. Therefore, the potential for increasing the number of bachelor's and graduate degrees among Mexican Americans is tangible. Nevertheless, persistent gaps remain in achievement between Mexican Americans and other major racial/ethnic groups in higher education outcomes such as bachelor's and graduate degree completion. Without addressing the underlying causes of gaps in achievement, more college-age Mexican Americans will not necessarily help increase the proportion of Mexican Americans graduating from college or reach parity with other racial/ethnic groups.

Although college enrollment rates have been increasing for Latinos, a gap remains for Mexican American college-age youth. Based on data from the Pew Hispanic Center that disaggregated Latino subgroups, table 7 shows that about 18 percent of Mexican Americans aged eighteen to twenty-four years old (the typical college-age group) are enrolled in college in comparison to about 37 percent of college-age Whites (Fry, 2002).

The gap is partly attributable to the lower rate of high school completion for Mexican Americans. However, even among those who complete

Table 7. Undergraduate Enrollment Among Eighteen- to Twenty-Four-Year-Olds, by Race/Ethnicity, 1997–2000

	PERCENTAGE OF POPULATION	PERCENTAGE OF HIGH SCHOOL GRADUATES
Mexican	17.6	31.1
White	36.8	42.4
Black	28.3	37.2
Asian/Pacific Islander	50.4	56.9

Source: Fry, 2002, table 7

high school, the college enrollment rate is lower for Mexican Americans than for their White peers. Table 7 also shows that even among high school graduates, a gap remains. Thirty-one percent of Mexican Americans who have completed high school enroll in college, compared to 42 percent of Whites.

In addition to a lower rate of college enrollment, Mexican Americans lag behind other groups in attaining bachelor's and graduate degrees. Nine percent of Mexican Americans older than age twenty-five hold at least a bachelor's degree, compared to 28 percent of the overall U.S. population (Motel & Patten, 2012b; Ryan & Siebens, 2012). The low rate of college degree completion among Mexican Americans, like college enrollment, may be partly attributable to the lack of academic preparation for college work and the lower rate of completing high school than those of other major racial/ethnic groups.

Generational and Gender Differences in Higher Education

There are also important bachelor's degree attainment differences within the Mexican American population. For example, college enrollment differs among Mexican Americans depending on their generation in the United States. Among eighteen- to twenty-four-year-old high school graduates, about 21 percent of foreign-born Mexican Americans are enrolled in college, compared to 43 percent of second-generation and 34 percent of third-generation Mexican Americans (Fry, 2002). Notable is that while foreign-born Mexican American students fare poorly in comparison to second-generation students, third-generation students do not fare as well as second-generation students. Some scholars (e.g., Kao &

Tienda, 1995) contend that second-generation youth benefit in school from their immigrant parents' high optimism and work ethic, while the third generation does not. Third-generation students seemingly should benefit in school attainment from their English dominance and familiarity with the American schooling system, but this is not reflected in their college enrollment.

Another difference within the Mexican American population is that proportionally Mexican American female students have increasingly outpaced males in the last three decades in college attendance and degree attainment (this is true of females overall in the college-age population). In 2006, males represented only about 37 percent of Mexican American students entering four-year higher education institutions (Hurtado, Saenz, Santos, & Cabrera, 2008). Likewise, Latinas have outpaced Latinos in bachelor's degree completion. Latinas earn 4.2 percent of all bachelor's degrees versus 2.6 percent for Latinos (Gándara, 2009). Saenz and Ponjuan (2008) suggest that a combination of factors may be contributing to this gendered phenomenon, including sociocultural factors (e.g., cultural and gender norms or expectations), peer dynamics, and labor force demands. They have called the trend of the "vanishing Latino male" in higher education an epidemic that for the most part has been ignored and needs to be urgently addressed.

Factors Affecting Higher Education

Aspiring to go to college is a critical factor affecting college attendance for all students. It is not, however, the only factor that affects attendance. Although Mexican American students aspire to attend college, many factors impede their ability to attend and persist in higher education, including a lack of adequate academic preparation in K–12, the costs of college, the need to work, part-time attendance, and primarily being first-generation college students (for research and reviews of the literature see Chavez, 2008; Moore & Shulock, 2007; Ornelas & Solórzano, 2004; Rendon, Justiz, & Resta, 1988; Rivas, Perez, Alvarez, & Solórzano, 2007; Swail, Cabrera, & Lee, 2004).

Mexican American students are less likely to have the academic preparation necessary for college-level work. They are more likely to attend high-poverty and racially segregated K–12 schools and, consequently, are less likely to have access to rigorous academic preparation for college. Even in racially integrated schools, however, Mexican Americans are less likely to have a college preparatory curriculum. As discussed in more detail in chapter 2, Mexican American students are underrepresented in honors, AP, or other advanced programs like GATE or Magnet. As high school graduates, then, Mexican American students are less likely to have taken the coursework necessary for college admission, less likely to have covered rigorous academic material, and less likely to have developed the kinds of study and cognitive skills necessary for the college classroom, including critical and analytic thinking and problem solving. In one study using data from the National Center for Education Statistics, about 56 percent of Latino students were considered not qualified for college, and 17 percent were considered minimally qualified. In comparison, about 39 percent of their White peers were considered not qualified and 14 percent minimally qualified (Swail et al., 2004).

Even Mexican American students who complete high school and are considered college-bound are not as college-ready as their peers. They have less academic preparation, hurting their chances of college success. For example, College Board (2009) data on students who have taken the Scholastic Aptitude Test (SAT) show that Mexican Americans in comparison to White students are less likely to have taken calculus (22 percent versus 30 percent) and English honors courses (38 percent versus 43 percent) and more likely to have a lower high school GPA (3.22 versus 3.40). Mexican American college-bound students also have lower SAT scores in comparison to White students in all three areas: critical reading, mathematics, and writing. These college-readiness gaps may be even more severe because these statistics include only students who have taken the SAT. Many Mexican American students may not take the SAT because they have not been guided by their school to take it, have received no encouragement or mixed messages about attending college, or because it is not required for admittance to community colleges where they are more likely to attend if they go to college.

Mexican American students are also less likely to have the financial resources to support their college education. Mexican American students likely come from families with lower median household incomes than their White peers, affecting their ability to finance their education. Consequently, Mexican American students are likely to choose the least expensive avenues for a college education; they are more likely to choose less selective public institutions, especially two-year public schools. Unfortunately, students who attend these types of schools have reduced chances of completing a bachelor's degree. Moreover, a lack of financial resources for Mexican American students brings with it the need to work. Mexican American students are more likely to work while in college and assist in supporting their family. Since working may be necessary for most Mexican American college students, they have less time available for rigorous study, research for class or with faculty, and participating in college activities and support groups that help to keep students in school. Mexican American college students are also more likely to attend college on a part-time basis in order to maintain a job to support their schooling; this contributes to a weaker connection between students and college attendance.

Finally, Mexican Americans are largely first-generation college students, meaning that they are often the first in their families to navigate a complex higher educational system. Of high school seniors who took the SAT, 71 percent of Mexican Americans were first-generation college students as compared to 28 percent of their White peers (College Board, 2009). While first-generation Mexican American students may have the support of their parents and family, they are not as likely to have family and friends with social capital such as specific knowledge, resources, and networks necessary for success in college (e.g., knowing the requirements for a bachelor's degree or how to apply for financial aid or other forms of financial support). They are also less likely to attend schools that provide necessary institutional supports such as consistent and appropriate counseling and college workshops. However, even when schools provide some academic support for college preparation, first-generation college students struggle with understanding how the higher education system works, what resources are available, and how they can access those resources and use them to their advantage. They are literally learning as they go, and this makes for a college road filled with speed bumps, detours, and, for many students, dead ends. Moreover, first-generation students may feel alone in their college journey, both when not many other students from their school or community have taken the college path and when the college attended has students of racial, ethnic, and/or social class backgrounds that do not match their own. Additionally, many college campuses do not meet the cultural needs of first-generation working-class Mexican American students, often contributing to feelings of alienation on campus. Feelings of not "belonging" compounded with a lack of social capital make the journey difficult for first-generation students.

Additional Hurdles for Undocumented Students

I felt so bad! Because my friends knew my grades and they would ask me, "What school did you apply to?" And I was like, "No, I didn't." "How come you haven't applied?!" . . . And one friend, she knew about my situation and she said, "You know what? I feel so bad because your grades are much better than mine and I'm able to go to a university and you're not." I felt like crying. . . . All they do senior year is talk about college. "I applied here and I applied there" and I didn't even bother applying because I knew the answer—I couldn't pay for it. (Undocumented youth comment, Abrego, 2008, p. 718)

A range of issues can impede college attendance and degree completion for Mexican American students. Undocumented students have additional burdens in pursuing higher education (Abrego, 2008; Covarrubias & Lara, 2014; Oliverez, 2006a; Perez Huber, Malagon, & Solórzano, 2009). In the last few decades, a strong anti-immigrant and anti-Mexican and Latino sentiment in the United States has led to legislation restricting access to higher education for undocumented students. While attempts to restrict access to free K–12 public education have been rejected by the courts (see *Plyler v. Doe*, 1982, and California Proposition 187), access to higher education for undocumented immigrant students has not been fully supported and varies by state.

Several court rulings and legislative statutes have affected the ability of undocumented students to go to college. The focus of these legal wranglings has been on whether undocumented immigrant students should pay tuition as in-state residents or as out-of-state residents and on their eligibility for government financial aid. While most states grant admission of undocumented students to colleges (with the exceptions of Alabama and South Carolina), currently only about seventeen allow in-state tuition eligibility. This is a major issue because the difference between in-state and out-of-state tuition for an academic year in college can be tens of thousands of dollars. For example, the difference between in-state and out-of-state tuition and fees for flagship universities nationally varies considerably, $7,963 versus $21,215, respectively (Washington Higher Education Coordinating Board, 2010). This cost difference is a large impediment to pursing higher education for undocumented students.

Access to state financial aid is even more limited than access to in-state tuition; only California, Minnesota, New Mexico, Texas, and Washington currently allow state financial aid for undocumented students. In 2001, Texas passed a bill (HB 1403) that allowed undocumented students eligibility for in-state tuition and state financial aid. This was followed by New Mexico's passage of SB 582 in 2005. In 2011, California Assembly Bills 130 and 131 allowed undocumented students eligibility for state financial aid. Most recently (in 2013 and 2014, respectively), the states of Minnesota and Washington passed legislation allowing state financial aid. Despite efforts by this handful of states, a lack of state and federal financial aid is a major obstacle to higher education for undocumented students (Oliverez, 2006b; Perez Huber et al., 2009).

Across the nation, undocumented students remain in a tenuous and contentious position in their ability to access higher education due to state differences in legislation. While prior versions of the federal Dream Act would have allowed all states (on a voluntary basis) to charge undocumented students in-state tuition, that part of the legislation was eliminated. In 2012, the Deferred Action for Childhood Arrivals (DACA) passed, permitting undocumented youth who had arrived in the United States before age sixteen (and meeting other criteria) a temporary suspension of deportation and authorization to work. While not a path to citizenship, it allows for some social and economic incorporation of youth.

While the financial barrier is a large obstacle that students may try to overcome by working longer hours, taking more units than desirable, and applying for scholarships without citizenship requirements, there is also an emotional toll for students who feel alone and ostracized in American society and demoralized about their futures. Nevertheless, one study of undocumented youth found that AB 540 in California (allowing in-state tuition) had unintentionally reduced the stigma of being undocumented by providing a new neutral identity as an "AB 540 student," which also provided a sense of societal legitimacy. Additionally, undocumented students who, before AB 540, had hidden or expressed shame for their status were empowered to identify themselves in order to find and organize with similar students to garner and disseminate information specific to their status and to mobilize to claim and request rights (Abrego, 2008). Recognizing the educational rights of undocumented students is an important step in the legal and political legitimization of their status in American society, opening social, political, and economic doors. More importantly, it recognizes the human rights of all individuals in American society.

Anti–Affirmative Action Court Cases and Legislation

In the last few decades, several court rulings have eliminated affirmative action policies that have helped provide access to higher education for Mexican Americans since the 1960s. The impact of poverty, inferior school conditions, segregation, curriculum tracking, and low expectations for Mexican American students has affected their ability to attend higher education. Initially, affirmative action was meant to address past and current discrimination impeding the occupational mobility of ethnic and racial minorities. Affirmative action was established in 1961 by President Kennedy's issuance of Executive Order 10925 to prohibit government contractors from discriminating on the basis of race, creed, color, or national origin. Later, women were also included in affirmative action legislation through Executive Order 11375 and Title IX of the Educational Amendments of 1972. Colleges and universities joined in this effort to provide access to these groups. Since these policies began, the representation of Latinos on college campuses has increased, as has the number of degree holders (Charleston, 2009).

Despite these gains, support for affirmative action policies has not been universal. Critics claim that affirmative action is reverse discrimination or that these policies are not necessary because racial discrimination no longer exists in American society. Advocates, on the other hand, claim that affirmative action is necessary to address systemic discrimination against Mexican Americans and other people of color. State courts and the Supreme Court have attempted to tackle various challenges to the constitutionality of affirmative action in higher education (for a full discussion of affirmative action in higher education, see *Mexican Americans and the Law* in this textbook series).

In *Regents of the University of California v. Bakke* (1978), one of the first cases to challenge affirmative action, the plaintiff claimed reverse discrimination in the University of California Davis's Medical School admissions process due to its affirmative action policy. The plaintiff was a white male who was denied admission to the school. At issue were the sixteen of one hundred admission slots the school set aside for students of color. The Supreme Court ruled that while "quotas" were unconstitutional based on the Fourteenth Amendment's Equal Protection Clause, a state could use race as one factor in admissions to promote educational diversity.

Equal protection under the Fourteenth Amendment and whether achieving diversity in higher education is a compelling state interest have remained key issues in affirmative action challenges since the *Bakke* case. Additional strikes against affirmative action were *Hopwood v. Texas* (1996) and SP-1 and Proposition 209 in California. In the *Hopwood* case, affirmative action in higher education was struck down by the Fifth Circuit in Texas, Louisiana, and Mississippi. The court's opinion was that race could not be used in university admissions due to the Fourteenth Amendment. However, the *Hopwood* decision was later repealed by *Grutter v. Bollinger* (2003).

In 1996, SP-1 at the University of California (UC) also ended affirmative action policies in their admissions process. Although SP-1 was later rescinded, California Proposition 209 continued this action by prohibiting public institutions, including higher education institutions, from using race, sex, or ethnicity in admissions or for consideration. Since SP-1 and Proposition 209, the admission of Latino students to the University of California system has been severely affected. In 1998, the first year affected by Proposition 209, 53 percent fewer Latinos were admitted to UC Berkeley and 33 percent fewer to UC Los Angeles than the previous year (Gándara, 1999b). Underrepresentation of Latinos continues throughout the UC system. In 2006, while more than 50 percent of K–12 students in California were Latino, this group made up only 13 percent of UC students (Chacon, 2008). Thus, a major concern is that while Latinos represent increasing proportions of high school graduates, their underrepresentation in the UC system is worsened due to anti–affirmative action rulings.

Three affirmative action cases in Michigan and Texas show that the issue of affirmative action has not been resolved. In *Grutter v. Bollinger* (2003) and *Gratz v. Bollinger* (2003), the University of Michigan School of Law and undergraduate admissions policies, respectively, were challenged due to race-conscious admissions policies used in pursuit of diverse classes. Again, the argument was that race-conscious admissions were a violation of the Equal Protection Clause of the Fourteenth Amendment. In *Grutter*, the Supreme Court ruled that the University of Michigan Law School could use race as one of several factors in admissions because student body diversity is a compelling state interest. Additionally, as long as the process was "narrowly tailored" to achieve student diversity, it was constitutional. In *Gratz*, the admissions process was challenged due to extra points (20) awarded to underrepresented students or students from predominantly minority or disadvantaged schools. In this case, the Supreme Court ruled that the admissions process was not narrowly customized to achieve the university's desired goal of a diverse student body and was, therefore, unconstitutional. Most recently, in *Fisher v. University of Texas at Austin* (2013), a race-conscious admissions process was again challenged. Although use of race as one factor in admissions was not ruled unconstitutional, the Supreme Court sent the case back to a lower court because in the higher court's opinion the lower court did not use "strict scrutiny" in assessing the university's use of race in admissions to determine if it was "narrowly tailored" and necessary to promote a diverse student body.

Overall, using race as one factor in university admissions to foster diversity has been generally supported by court cases, while creating slots or quotas based on race has been declared unconstitutional. After the *Hopwood* decision in Texas and the passage of Proposition 209 in California, both states developed alternative plans to try to maintain a diverse student body, which included guaranteed admission for the top students from each high school in the state (Texas) or from the state as a whole (California). Nevertheless, some research has shown that these states experienced decreased applications to and enrollment in college from Latino and other students of color (Charleston, 2009). As evidenced in California and Texas, the anti–affirmative action legislation that has followed in numerous other states (e.g., Washington, Michigan, Nebraska) may have detrimental effects on the already underrepresented population of Mexican American students in state universities. Proponents of affirmative action argue that purportedly race-blind policies do not address the results of past discrimination and current unequal school conditions for Mexican American students. Moreover, addressing these unequal school conditions and developing viable outreach and recruitment plans to maintain diversity in higher education is critical so that Mexican Americans and other students of color are able to participate fully in higher education and all sectors of the labor market.

Community College: Open Doorway and Dead End

When I started community college, I absolutely did not know what I was doing. I didn't know what else to do after graduating from high school and so I followed my brother to our local community college. When I first got there, I had never heard of a bachelor's or any other type of degree. I really didn't know what college was for, but not knowing what else to do, I kept plowing along. Somewhere along the path, I focused on getting a one-semester certificate as some sort of business secretary, and, eventually, I think in my second or third year there, I heard about something called "transferring." That became my new goal. (Estela, author of this text and former first-generation college student)

Mexican American students are much more likely than students of other racial/ethnic groups to begin their college education at community colleges. Research shows that about 42 percent of Mexican American students enrolled in higher education attend a two-year community college instead of a four-year institution. This compares with about 24 percent of their White peers who start at a two-year institution (Fry, 2002). Other research has found even higher rates of enrollment (more than two-thirds) at two-year institutions among Mexican Americans attending college (Nuñez & Crisp, 2012; Yosso & Solorzano, 2006). The large proportion of Mexican Americans who begin college at community colleges may be due to a combination of factors, including lower costs, proximity to home, class times that accommodate working students, availability of basic-skills classes, and ease of admittance. Nevertheless, the majority of Mexican American students who begin at community college aspire to transfer to a four-year institution to obtain a baccalaureate degree (Rendon & Nora, 1997).

Due to the large proportion of Mexican American students who begin at community colleges, one area of concern has centered on whether community colleges adequately support students, particularly students of color, in transferring to four-year institutions. On the one hand, the percentage of students who transfer from community college to four-year institutions is dismally low. On the other, for many Mexican American students who attain undergraduate degrees, community college is where they began. Research has shown that even for Mexican American doctoral students, 23 percent attended community college, more than any other racial/ethnic group (Rivas et al., 2007). Thus, while community colleges represent an important avenue for advancing the educational goals of Mexican American students, unfortunately, they also represent significant risk for those who begin their higher education path there. Latino students are more likely to drop out of college if they begin their studies at a community college. One study showed attrition rates as high as 80 percent for Latino students in community college (Rendon & Nora, 1989, as cited in Martinez &

Fernández, 2004). Additionally, the main goal of Latino community college students—transferring to a four-year institution for at least a baccalaureate degree—is achieved at a low rate. Another study found that of Chicana/o students who start at community college, only one of seventeen transfers to a four-year university (Yosso, 2006). Transfer rates from community college are low for all students and Mexican Americans in particular.

Overall, students who attend community college in comparison to those who attend four-year institutions have characteristics that put them in a precarious educational position. Research has found that community college students are more likely to come from low-income households, be minority, be first-generation, be older than average college students, have children, be a single parent, delay enrollment after high school, work, and have had lower achievement in high school (see, e.g., Horn, Nevill, & Griffith, 2006; Nuñez & Crisp, 2012). These risk factors can negatively affect continued enrollment in community college and degree attainment.

While there are many challenges for Mexican American community college students, institutional issues specific to community colleges can also impede the transition to a four-year institution. One criticism of community colleges is a lack of commitment to and full support for their transfer function. Some research indicates that community colleges have put more emphasis on vocational training as opposed to preparing students to transfer to a four-year institution. The high proportion of Mexican American college students that aspire to transfer, and even those undecided, need community colleges that have strong support for transferring to a four-year institution.

Developing the Transfer Function and a Transfer Culture

Researchers have suggested institutional solutions to issues facing Latino community college students (Martinez & Fernández, 2004; Moore & Shulock, 2007; Ornelas, 2002; Ornelas & Solórzano, 2004; Rivas et al., 2007; Suarez, 2003). Given that community colleges are the primary avenue for Latino students pursuing higher education, a major goal must be to transfer community college students to four-year institutions. In part, this would include the seemingly simple goal of providing all students with accurate information on transferring. Research has shown that inaccurate information or unclear instructions on transferring pose barriers for community college students (Ornelas, 2002). Other scholars recommend strengthening the relationship between community colleges and four-year institutions to ensure outreach, mentorship, recruitment, enrollment, and retention of community college students (Rivas et al., 2007). Improving the transfer function would, thus, be one way to address the paradox between the large portions of Latino community college students who want to transfer to a four-year institution and the extremely low transfer rates to such institutions.

Ornelas and Solórzano (2004) suggest multifaceted institutional changes to develop a "transfer culture" and improve academic conditions for Latino community college students. They suggest that each stakeholder (administrators, counselors, faculty, and students) has a role in creating the optimal conditions to facilitate transferring from community college. For example, administrators should create a computer-based system to keep students and counselors informed of course requirements met or needed, fund programs for learning communities, and provide more financial aid assistance. Counselors, for their part, should provide all students with essential transfer information, require counselor visits to develop educational plans, and establish courses or other outreach services that provide information on transferring and financial aid. Students must also take an active role in seeking information about the transfer process and any support services on campus that assist students in dealing with outside responsibilities. Moreover, Ornelas and Solórzano (2004) suggest that to develop an effective transfer function, college personnel must know the needs of the particular students they serve (e.g., providing support services for students who need to take evening courses), and all aspects of the transfer function should seek to address those needs.

Other Institutional Supports

A number of studies have also pointed to Mexican American– or Latino-centered or -inclusive support services such as summer bridge programs, clubs, and sororities or fraternities that serve as academic and social support mechanisms. Many of these groups and programs are founded on meeting the needs of Latino or underrepresented students. These groups and programs can be major-specific (such as the Society of Hispanics in Science and Engineering and the Latino Student Business Association) or geared toward specific subgroups such as women, men, Mexican Americans, or Latinos in general. They serve to provide college information such as where to go for assistance with degree requirements, financial aid, and academic advising. Some programs begin before college—targeting middle and high school students—to start providing information about and support for college as early as possible. For example, the Department of Education's GEAR UP begins support in middle school for students and their families. The Puente Project, a state-funded California-based program, focuses on supporting college attendance among high school and community college students. The program aims to provide students with the skills, knowledge, attitudes, and resources for college attendance. Research has shown that in high school, Puente Project students benefit from improved academics as well as high educational aspirations, positive attitudes toward schooling, knowledge about applying to college, and valuing an identity as a "good student" (Gándara, 1999b, 2005). Additionally, the various programs and clubs play an important role in providing a support network of Latino students and faculty who can provide camaraderie, empathy, and mentoring. All of these groups and programs help to combat a sense of confusion, isolation, and feelings of not belonging.

Staying in and Moving up the Pipeline: Graduate Degrees

Each step in the educational pipeline affects the next level, and students cannot jump ahead in the pipeline without completing the requisite requirements. Thus, graduating from high school affects college attendance and bachelor's degree attainment, and bachelor's degree completion, in turn, affects pursuing graduate or professional studies. **Postbaccalaureate** studies are important because advanced degrees are necessary for many leadership and decision-making positions in society. These may include law and medical degrees, PhDs, and a wide variety of master's degrees such as MBAs, MFAs, and MSWs. There is also great financial gain over a lifetime for those with advanced degrees. With advanced degrees, Mexican Americans can participate fully in all aspects of a democratic society.

Even though Mexican American students may have made it to college in pursuit of their bachelor's degree, challenges in continuing on to advanced studies may remain. These challenges include lack of information and encouragement to pursue postbaccalaureate studies, financial aid, role models, mentoring by faculty members, and research experience. Additionally, other challenges include family responsibilities, stigmatization

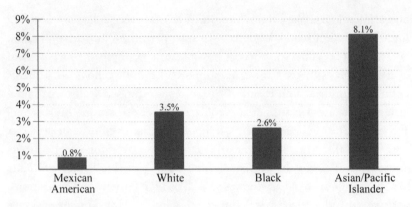

Figure 13. Graduate school enrollment among twenty-five- to thirty-four-year-olds, by race/ethnicity. Source: Adapted from Fry (2002), table 7.

as affirmative action students, and racial and gender discrimination (D. G. Solórzano, 1993).

Mexican Americans have the lowest rate of graduate school enrollment of any major racial/ethnic group. Figure 13 shows the graduate school enrollment rate for Mexican Americans and other major racial/ethnic groups. Pew Hispanic Center data show that among twenty-five- to thirty-four-year-olds, 0.8 percent of Mexican Americans are enrolled in graduate school, compared to 3.5 percent of their White peers. The low rate of graduate school enrollment for Mexican Americans is affected by their low rate of bachelor's degree attainment (Fry, 2002).

Given the low rates of graduate school enrollment for all races, it is not unexpected that at the doctoral level, Mexican American students are underrepresented. Using age cohort averages from 1990 to 2000, National Opinion Research Center and U.S. Census data show that Mexican American women in the typical age range for receiving a doctoral degree (thirty to thirty-four years old) were 6.7 percent of the female population; however, they represented only 1.1 percent of female doctorate recipients. Faring worse, Mexican American males were 7.9 percent of the male population but only 1 percent of male doctorate recipients (D. G. Solórzano, Rivas, & Velez, 2005). To achieve parity, Mexican American females and males would have to increase doctorate production by about 600 percent and 700 percent, respectively. In addition to the low percentages of Mexican American students pursuing doctoral degrees, those who obtain their doctorate are not equally represented in all fields of study. Mexican American doctorates are less likely to be in physical sciences, engineering, life sciences, humanities, and other professional fields in comparison to education and social science fields (D. G. Solórzano, 1993; D. G. Solórzano et al., 2005).

Factors Affecting Graduate School Success

For most students, completing an advanced degree is a difficult path to navigate that requires persistence and diligence. Research has identified significant factors that affect the graduate school experiences of Latino students, including family support, financial aid, campus climate, and role models or mentors (Perez Huber, Huidor, Malagon, Sanchez, & Solórzano, 2006). Since Latino students often are the first in their families to pursue a college education, and especially an advanced degree, family support is critical. One study of high-achieving Mexican Americans who pursued advanced degrees found that they attributed their drive in school to parents (especially mothers) who cultivated a "culture of possibility" (Gándara, 1995). In this study, parents—who overwhelmingly had low levels of education—emphasized high academic aspirations for their children and strove to provide them with the best schools and programs available. Moreover, even though Mexican American parents with low levels of education often may not be able to provide specific knowledge or advice about navigating undergraduate and graduate school, they can provide a source of encouragement and emotional support. For married Mexican American students, spousal support is also important for graduate studies.

Research has also shown that financial aid is critical for Latino students pursuing graduate or professional education. Financial assistance can play a deciding factor in whether to pursue an advanced degree. In one study of Chicanas who were either in or had completed a doctoral program, a respondent commented that the "bottom line . . . was financial aid. No matter how smart or motivated I was, I couldn't have done it without the money that I've gotten" (Cúadraz, 1996, p. 215). Moreover, adequate funding allows students to work less and study more. If financial assistance is in the form of graduate assistantships, it provides opportunity to work with faculty on research or teaching.

Campus climate is also important for Latino students pursuing advanced degrees. Research has shown that racial and gender discrimination on campus can have a negative impact on students of color and women students. A negative campus climate can make Latino students feel out of place on campus or academically inferior. This can affect their academic self-concept, academic performance, and persistence. Some research has focused on the impact of racial **microaggressions**—commonplace humiliating subtle messages—on Latino undergraduate and graduate students (D. G. Solórzano, 1998; Yosso, Smith, Ceja, & Solórzano, 2009). For example, in a study of Chicana and Chicano scholars, three forms of racial and gender microaggressions emerged: feeling out of place at the university, lower expectations from faculty (e.g., for being a minority, coming from a low socioeconomic status, having an accent, and being a female), and racist/sexist attitudes and behaviors (D. G. Solórzano, 1998). Racial microaggressions can take the form of verbal and nonverbal racial insults from other campus members (including faculty and student peers), racial jokes, and an overall institutional atmosphere that makes Latino students feel unwelcome or out of place. Each of these, if occurring often enough, can contribute to a sense of self-doubt, isolation, and discouragement. Mexican American graduate students may begin to doubt their academic abilities and the worthiness of their scholarly contributions, which may cause them to reevaluate seeking a graduate degree.

Finally, having role models or mentors is also important for Latino graduate students. Research has found that it is important to identify faculty advisors who can provide assistance with academic advice, financial information, and emotional support for Latino students. In one study on Mexican American doctorate recipients, positive mentoring relationships were mentioned by students as the single most important factor in obtaining their doctoral degree (D. G. Solórzano, 1993). As one postdoctoral student commented in a study on Chicana and Chicano scholars, "Role models are important because you need to see someone like you in the position that you hope to attain. Otherwise you began to wonder, to doubt, to second guess yourself" (D. G. Solórzano, 1998, p. 128). Again, because Mexican American students are often the first in their families to navigate advanced education and may feel isolated (e.g., culturally, socioeconomically), faculty guidance or guidance from others who have taken a similar educational path is critical for graduate school success.

Family and schooling background have also been found to support academic success at the highest level. In Gándara's (1995) study of Mexican American MDs, JDs, and PhDs from low-income backgrounds, factors important to their academic success included a high value placed on literacy, attending desegregated schools, coming from a household that placed a strong emphasis on hard work, and communication of family stories and legends that provided hope for future success. Parents who read the Bible, newspapers, and books; bought costly encyclopedias for their children;

worked hard at low-skill jobs (thus modeling a work ethic for children to strive hard in school); and told stories of family heroes who represented hope for the children about the future were all part of these high-achieving Mexican Americans' upbringing. Additionally, high-achieving participants were sent by their parents (and sometimes by themselves) to desegregated schools with White or highly mixed student bodies where they were able to access a college preparatory curriculum, take advantage of social capital from students who helped to navigate the school system toward a college path, and develop an ability to cross cultural borders that could be used in higher education institutions.

Women and Racial and Gender Microaggressions

While the aforementioned factors affect all Mexican Americans, research shows gender differences in how these factors in higher education are experienced. Mexican American females are more likely than men to experience racial and gender discrimination in pursing their undergraduate and graduate studies (D. G. Solórzano, 1993). The discrimination may come from professors, administration, staff, and other students. Some discrimination comes in the form of gender stereotyping. In one study, a Mexican American female commented that questions asked prior to being admitted to a doctoral program were about if she "was going to get married, have a baby, etc. [She] had to convince them [she] would not drop out of graduate school" (Achor & Morales, 1990, p. 278). Some studies found that other forms of racial and gender discrimination may include unwanted touching or jokes and patronizing or condescending behaviors toward Mexican American female graduate students.

Resilience and Resistance

> I can't be a quitter. I can't quit, because then I'm just reinforcing the stereotypes they have of us anyway. So I just kept going. (doctoral student; Cúadraz, 1996, p. 219)

Many scholars have written about the resilience of Mexican American students that allows them to pursue, persist in, and graduate from college. As discussed earlier, many studies have identified familial support as a key factor. Likewise, financial support, mentorship, and supportive friends or groups are critical. Additionally, some Mexican American students are also motivated to "prove the messages wrong" or "prove them wrong" (Achor & Morales, 1990; Talavera-Bustillos, 1998, 2007; Yosso, 2000, 2006). That is, Mexican American students can be motivated to go to college or persist in college to counter negative messages they have received about their academic and college-going abilities. Sometimes the negative messages come from nonsupportive family members or school personnel. For Mexican American women, these messages can be intertwined with rigid gender expectations about marriage and childbearing. In one study, a brother responded to his high school sister's expressed desire to attend college by stating, "Why are you going to school if you're going to end up pregnant and married anyway?" She in turn concluded,

> Maybe he didn't think much of it, but I did. I really took it seriously; I took it to the heart. At that time, I think I had … I had sent my application already for the [university], and I'm, like, this is the school I had my heart set on, so when he told me that, I was, like, "Damn!" you know. It was a hard time. It was like one little comment can really hurt you. Yeah, I told him … "You don't know! I am going to finish high school and go to college." (Interview; Talavera-Bustillos, 2007, p. 459)

While obviously hurt by her brother's comments about her assumed life path as a woman, this student's determination to succeed in her college plans intensified. Scholars identify the motivation to "prove them wrong" as a form of student resistance that rejects negative racial/ethnic and/or gender messages conveyed to them and fortifies them to counter those messages by persisting and working harder toward their academic goals.

Research has also found that while Latino students may experience a negative racial climate in college, they respond by community building and developing critical navigation skills (Yosso et al., 2009). Latino students build a sense of community by joining or creating academic and social counterspaces that affirm their cultural knowledge such as clubs, campus cultural centers, and outreach programs. They also develop critical navigation skills by learning to seek out affirming counterspaces and then using those navigation skills to either "give back" or assist their communities or families. For example, in Cúadraz's (1996) study of Mexican American women who had gone through doctoral programs, the formation of Chicana academic support groups was important for coping with marginalization in graduate school. Additionally, many of the women saw their persistence at the university from a political perspective—their presence and critical voices were needed to advocate for other Mexican American women.

In negative campus climates, attitudes and messages can affect students in harmful ways. However, resistance to these attitudes and messages can be transformational. Transformational resistance means that Mexican American students become aware and critical of social oppression and are motivated by an interest in social justice (D. G. Solórzano & Delgado Bernal, 2001). Therefore, even though students may feel as though they do not belong at the university, they begin to understand that inequalities in the larger society (e.g., in K–12 education, the labor market, and the political system) are the root of problems at the university level and that they themselves are not the problem, even though they may have been made to feel that way. They are motivated to continue on in school because they are aware of this, to help others like themselves who are negatively affected by these conditions, and to work to eradicate oppressive conditions on campus or in the larger society. D. G. Solórzano and Delgado Bernal (2001) state, "With a deeper level of understanding and a social justice orientation, transformational resistance offers the greatest possibility for social change" (p. 319).

Concluding Thoughts

Increased enrollment in and graduation from college is an important goal for Mexican American students, both for themselves and for realizing the larger democratic goal of equality of opportunity for all. Some of the challenges to higher education for Mexican American students begin earlier in the educational pipeline. Of primary importance, the lack of academic preparation for college-level work in high school and the high push-out/dropout rate of Mexican American high school students affect the proportion of this group continuing on to college. Even when Mexican American students attend college, many factors affect their persistence and graduation rate, such as finances and campus climate. While community college is an important avenue to higher education for Mexican American students, it also has many areas that need strengthening in order to support transition to four-year universities. Boosting undergraduate and graduate school attendance and graduation is critical to Mexican Americans playing important roles in all sectors of American society. Mexican American students have shown resilience and resistance in navigating higher education but, nevertheless, need support in accomplishing their educational goals.

Discussion Exercises

1. Identify and discuss four factors that impede higher education for Mexican American students. Suggest how these factors can be addressed.

2. Why are finances a critical issue confronting undocumented students who attend college? What might be additional issues for undocumented students in or after college?

3. Why does the author refer to community college as both an "open doorway and dead end"? Do you agree or disagree? Why?

4. Discuss the arguments for and against affirmative action. Do you think Mexican Americans still need affirmative action? Why or why not?

5. List three factors affecting graduate school attendance. Discuss specific scenarios (life examples) for how each factor can affect a student. Choose one factor and develop a skit that demonstrates that factor's negative and/or positive results.

6. How is "prove them wrong" a form of resistance? What strategies do students use to resist negative messages and climate?

Suggested Readings

Castellanos, J., Gloria, A. M., & Kamimura, M. (2006). *The Latina/o pathway to the Ph.D.: Abriendo caminos.* Sterling, VA: Stylus Pub.

Fry, R. (2002). *Latinos in higher education: Many enroll, too few graduate.* Washington, DC: Pew Hispanic Center.

Gándara, P. (1995). *Over the ivy walls: The educational mobility of low-income Chicanos.* Albany: State University of New York Press.

Gándara, P. (1999). Staying in the race: The challenge for Chicanos/as in higher education. In J. F. Moreno (Ed.), *The elusive quest for equality: 150 years of Chicano/Chicana education* (pp. 169–96). Cambridge, MA: Harvard Educational Review.

Swail, W. S., Cabrera, A. F., & Lee, C. I. (2004). *Latino youth and the pathway to college.* Washington, DC: Pew Hispanic Center.

Chapter 5

Recognizing Strengths and Promoting Strategies for Success

This text has discussed some of the major educational issues and outcomes for Mexican American students, such as standardized test scores, push-out rates, graduating from high school, and enrolling in college. Research shows that Mexican American students have not realized the same academic achievement as other U.S. racial and ethnic groups. Deficit thinking has often been used to understand the low achievement of Mexican American students. Whether it was due to genetic inferiority, a lack of cultural or familial values that emphasize education, or a lack of motivation or ability, low achievement has oftentimes been blamed on Mexican American students. Even though these negative beliefs about Mexican American educational achievement have been dominant in society, many scholars, educators, and community members reject using deficit thinking to understand Mexican Americans' educational achievement.

As discussed throughout this text, many factors, including school conditions and practices, have contributed to and perpetuated educational inequalities for Mexican American students. Institutional barriers (e.g., school segregation, curriculum tracking away from honors or AP programs and courses), educational policies (e.g., restrictive or inadequate language policies), politics, and racism and classism, among many factors, have played roles in the low achievement of Mexican American students. Acknowledging and examining factors such as these allows for a broader understanding of Mexican American education. Many educators and scholars have developed alternative theories and strategies that critique mainstream narratives and methods of providing education to improve educational achievement.

This chapter focuses on scholarship that critiques and provides a new understanding of power dynamics in society that disadvantage poor people and people of color. Additionally, this scholarship highlights the strengths of Mexican American students, families, and communities and the kinds of ideological, pedagogical, and institutional changes that support the educational success of Mexican American students. No one theory or model presented here purports to have a comprehensive answer to improve the educational outcomes for Mexican American students, but each strives to address specific issues considered important for their educational success (e.g., school organization, culturally relevant curriculum).

Critiques of Power

Chapter 1 discussed in detail the dominant theoretical framework of deficit thinking. Many theories have challenged this framework by focusing on alternative points of analysis. These theories have rejected the premise of deficit thinking that disenfranchised groups are themselves responsible for their low social statuses. Instead, these theories shed light on ideologies that uphold inequalities and allow them to remain unseen or legitimized. They provide a new lens that focuses on power relations in society and systems of domination such as racism, sexism, and classism. They propose that these power relations and systems of domination are integrated into the norms and institutions of society, and thus, recognizing inequality is difficult. Nevertheless, challenging inequality is possible and necessary for social justice.

Critical Theory

Critical theory is based on a critique of theories, such as reproduction theory (discussed in chapter 1), that strive to find all-encompassing explanations of unequal power dynamics in the world. Although critical theory, like reproduction theory, does view schools and other institutions as sites of struggle between dominant and disenfranchised groups, it does not view economic power as omnipotent or deterministic in structuring social and political relations. Schools are not viewed as sites where the dominant class has complete control of the destiny of marginalized groups. People, even from disenfranchised groups, are viewed as having human agency to resist oppressive conditions, thus enabling them to create change and transform society.

Critical theorists propose that despite incomplete control of disenfranchised groups, institutions such as schools uphold and reinforce the power of dominant groups through school rules, norms, and practices that favor them. These school conditions are presented as neutral and apolitical, which masks and mutes criticism of them. Critical theorists propose that in reality these school conditions work against disenfranchised groups in society because they perpetuate unequal opportunities and outcomes of schooling. For example, curriculum tracking or sorting students by their perceived abilities in school (discussed in chapter 2) is generally viewed as a normal, objective, and apolitical practice. It has been normalized because it has become fundamental in American schools and integrated into mainstream ideology as the "natural" way schooling should be done. The noncritical acceptance of this worldview is established through socialization.

Critical theorists, however, challenge the premise of neutrality and consider it part of a worldview upheld by those who benefit from it. They refer to this as hegemony. Therefore, in the example of curriculum tracking, schools perpetuate inequalities and disempower subordinate groups by disproportionately leaving them out of the highest tracks that provide a rigorous curriculum and preparation for college (e.g., AP or honors classes). This is aided by the use of standardized tests that are also uncritically accepted as making the sorting process fair.

Critical theorists propose that dominant groups also maintain power by controlling what is considered legitimate and correct knowledge. This is the knowledge that provides advantages and power in society, and therefore, disenfranchised groups have restricted access to it. In school, this has negative implications for subordinate groups of students because their knowledge is dismissed or excluded and access to knowledge considered legitimate is limited. A recent example is the banning of the Mexican American Studies program in Arizona in 2010. Despite increased high school graduation rates for students in the program, the program was banned because the curriculum challenged the dominant narrative of history, literature, and other disciplines by incorporating Mexican American–themed books, perspectives, and topics. The program was accused of promoting anti-American sentiments in students, simply by challenging what was considered legitimate knowledge.

Critical theory proposes that if subordinate classes develop awareness of oppressive conditions, they are able to use critically informed action to change these conditions. For example, the 1969 Walkouts in Crystal City, Texas (discussed in chapter 1), were led by students to change the conditions of their school that excluded their cultural background and limited access to school activities. In the case of Arizona's Mexican American Studies program ban, Mexican American students protested (including walkouts and sit-ins) and continue to work toward overturning the ban. Thus, critical theory is concerned with oppressive social conditions such as these and how people can work to transform unequal power structures in society to achieve social justice and human freedom. (Critical theory in education is discussed further in the Transformative Pedagogies section.)

Critical Race Theory and Latina(o) Critical Race Theory

Critical race theory (CRT) and Latina(o) Critical Race Theory (LatCrit) in education draw from and extend critical theory (Solórzano & Delgado Bernal, 2001). CRT and LatCrit focus on the persistence of race and racism in all sectors of American society. Based on the work of numerous scholars, Solórzano (1998) has identified five main tenets of CRT in education:

1. Race and racism are central, pervasive, and permanent components of U.S. society.
2. Mainstream claims of objectivity, meritocracy, color blindness, race neutrality, and equal opportunity in American society must be challenged.
3. For a socially just society, racism as well as other forms of subordination must be eliminated.
4. The experiential knowledge of people of color is "legitimate, appropriate, and critical to understanding, analyzing and teaching about racial subordination in the field of education" (p. 122).
5. Crossing disciplinary boundaries to study race and racism in education is necessary and must be done in both contemporary and historical analyses (see the works of Bell, 1992, 1995; Crenshaw, Gotanda, Peller, & Thomas, 1995; Delgado, 1995; and Matsuda, Lawrence, Delgado, & Crenshaw, 1993, for more depth from founding legal scholars).

These are also the principal tenets of LatCrit, although it focuses on Latina/o identity and their subordination and marginalization in school.

CRT and LatCrit in education use a race-conscious approach to analyze inequality in school. They propose that race is embedded in American beliefs and ideology and in educational structures, policies, and practice. While race is considered a social construct—that is, societies create its meaning—it has real-life consequences in everyday interactions with people and institutions (e.g., schools). Both theories also propose that race and racism intersect with other forms of subordination such as gender and social class. LatCrit also focuses on subordination by language, culture, immigration status, accent, phenotype, and sexual orientation. It emphasizes and illuminates the multidimensional and intersectional aspects of Latina/o identity and experience. For example, two Mexican American students may share some treatment as Mexican Americans in their school; however, if one identifies as lesbian, gay, bisexual, and transgender (LGBT) and the other as heterosexual, the socially subordinate status of being LGBT further affects the former person's status at the school. Thus, the student has the intersecting impact of being Mexican-origin and LGBT, which affects the student's daily life and social, economic, and political rights.

CRT and LatCrit do not view race and racism as exclusively historical but also as a contemporary phenomenon. In fact, analyzing historical racial oppression is fundamental to analyzing contemporary oppression. Furthermore, CRT and LatCrit challenge the ideology (neoliberalism) positing that racism is a historical aspect of American society (e.g., miscegenation laws) and is no longer important due to antidiscrimination laws passed in the last few decades. That is, due to racial integration and other civil rights laws of the 1950s and 1960s, neoliberalism purports that race no longer affects life experiences and opportunities in society, and therefore, there is no racial discrimination in schools. CRT and LatCrit oppose the tenets of this ideology and contend that the notion of a so-called colorblind society serves to mask contemporary racial inequalities and deny racial power dynamics that relegate people of color to the bottom. Instead, these theories propose that while there have been laws to address racial inequality, contemporary laws and institutional practices and policies are not race-neutral or objective. They propose that race and racism are still relevant in contemporary society. These are continuing issues because historical racial oppression (e.g., racial ideologies, laws, social norms) in various sectors of society, such as the educational system and labor market, contribute to contemporary inequality.

Due to the continuing relevance of race, CRT and LatCrit also posit that American meritocracy is a false ideology that serves as a façade to uphold unequal power and privilege. Meritocracy, like the achievement ideology for reproduction theory (see chapter 1), assumes that individual effort is the primary basis for future success, especially in school and work. Thus, if you are motivated and work hard, you achieve success; if you are unmotivated and do not work hard, you will not succeed. CRT and LatCrit challenge this ideology by proposing that the practices, policies, and structures of American society (along with other biases such as gender and social class) are not race-neutral and serve to reproduce racial inequalities that privilege Whites. In education, these embedded biases create an unequal playing field where students of color are at a disadvantage, regardless of their motivation and hard work. Like critical theory, however, CRT and LatCrit also propose that critically informed action by marginalized groups is always possible and necessary to move toward a socially just society.

Historically, the perspectives and knowledge of people of color and other subordinated groups have been excluded from or distorted in the practices, policies, and structures of American society. For example, the history and perspective of people of color in the United States had been largely ignored or told from an Anglo-centric perspective in history books and in the curriculum. These dominant narratives have controlled the storyline of history and been normalized. Therefore, they have been considered objective and apolitical. This becomes exceedingly evident when people of color or women challenge these narratives by creating new and alternative narratives and, consequently, are accused of bias and political motives. The bias and political nature of the dominant narrative had not been previously challenged (in a substantial way), and thus, to preserve power and discredit alternative narratives, these accusations emerge.

Due to exclusion and distortion in dominant narratives, CRT and LatCrit consider the voices or perspectives of subordinated groups essential for analyzing the educational system. Documenting their perspectives and insights is essential because these often counter dominant ideologies, thus revealing unequal conditions and treatment. For example, gaining insight about American society from a person with an accent and a third-grade education is just as important as, if not more important than, the insight from a highly educated, academic English–speaking person due to the former person's insights as someone with subordinate statuses in society. The former person is more likely to "see" and experience the impact of these subordinate statuses in his or her daily life. The subordinate statuses make inequality in society visible to this person because he or she experiences it in daily life (e.g., the assumption that a person with an accent or one with few years of schooling does not comprehend easily or thinks more slowly). Traditional academic research in education has often left out the perspectives and knowledge of students of color, instead leaving analysis and interpretation of educational issues to so-called experts. Therefore, CRT and LatCrit research approaches intentionally center the modes of communication and perspectives of people of color and Latinas/os to develop new narratives. These narratives may come in the forms of counterstories, poetry, fiction, and family histories; these are considered legitimate and necessary methods of information gathering.

Chicana Feminism

The 1960s were a time of civil rights and cultural nationalist movements, including the Chicano movement. While the Chicano movement was fighting against racial injustice in the larger society, its ideology did not recognize gender oppression. Consequently, Chicana feminism emerged, in part, in response to the patriarchal oppression of the Chicano movement. Chicana feminists were critical of the traditional gender roles within the movement that relegated them to subservient or auxiliary roles. Thus, Chicana feminism called for the recognition of racism and sexism as oppressive forces in the Chicano movement and society.

Chicana feminism offers a number of conceptual tools useful in educational institutions. As Chicana feminist theory and practice has developed over the decades (also called Chicana feminisms), it has recognized the multiple intersecting positions of Chicanas due to race, class, gender, sexuality, and nationality and the diversity of Chicana experiences. This position of hybridity (including bilingualism, biculturalism, biraciality) is one of strength to resist marginalization. This intersectionality is recognized as a "third space" from which Chicana feminists can offer critical insights and give voice to those silenced in various domains (Anzaldua, 1987; Perez, 1999; Sandoval, 2000). Chicana feminism(s) "constitute a political stance that confronts and undermines patriarchy as it cross-cuts forms of disempowerment and silencing such as racism, homophobia, class inequality, and nationalism" (Arredondo, 2003, p. 2).

Like previously discussed theories that critique power relations, Chicana feminism challenges what counts as knowledge and where it is produced. As a consequence, Chicana feminism respects and values the lived experiences and knowledge that Chicanas learn in their homes and community lives. These are strengths that help Chicanas navigate societal ideologies and institutions, including the educational institution and its norms, structures, and culture. Regarding higher education, Delgado Bernal (2006) states that "the communication, practices, and learning that occur in the home and community—what I call pedagogies of the home— often serve as a cultural knowledge base that helps Chicana students negotiate the daily experiences of sexist, racist and classist microaggressions" (p. 113). *Consejos* (advice) and storytelling are forms of cultural knowledge that provide strategies for resistance when obstacles are encountered in life, including the school context. A retold story of how *Abuelita* (grandmother) sneaked to school even though her mother forbade it because she was a girl can serve as a source of strength for a child to counter negative comments and experiences in school or sometimes from family members.

Dismissing negative comments and continuing to work hard in school without saying anything, voicing opposition and exposing repressive ideas, and forming a support group are forms of resistance that Chicanas can and do use. Chicana feminism identifies and gives a name and voice to Chicana resistance strategies invisible to or devalued by others. These positive strategies used to navigate the educational system have been called transformative resistance. Delgado Bernal (2006) states of transformative resistance:

> It is a resistance for liberation in which students are aware of social inequities and are motivated by emancipatory interests. The manifestations of transformational resistance can take on many forms—individual and subtle to collective and visible. Yet, when Chicana students engage in transformational resistance, they are opposing those ideas and ways of being that are disempowering to self. (p. 115)

Chicana feminism highlights Chicana agency in contesting unequal power relations, especially as they relate to race, gender, class, and sexual orientation and their intersections.

Redefining Capital

In the 1970s, French theorist Pierre Bourdieu (see Bourdieu & Passeron, 1977) developed the theoretical framework known as cultural reproduction (discussed in chapter 1), which examined the role of culture in the educational system. This model proposes that schools are set up to reward the cultural knowledge and skills of privileged groups in society. In this framework, middle- and upper-class cultural attributes are considered most valuable and useful for educational success. They serve as a form of capital or wealth, which supports advancement in schools. For example, students who speak a middle-class form of English are thought to have more valuable capital than students who speak a working-class form of English, because the middle-class form is what schools promote and reward. From the cultural reproduction perspective, schools recognize middle- and upper-class knowledge and skills as the normative knowledge and skills students should have, and they use these to measure academic achievement and as the basis for continued learning. In order to be successful in school, students must already have or acquire the knowledge and skills of those groups. However, access to these skills is limited, and as a consequence, students from marginal groups who bring alternative cultural capital to school are disadvantaged by school and may be less likely to be successful.

Bourdieu's cultural reproduction theory has been used to understand the low educational achievement of students of color and working-class and poor students. Applying the theory to many Mexican Americans who enter school speaking either Spanish or a nonstandard form of English (perhaps working-class or Chicano English) and/or have learned working-class values, it presumes they lack the appropriate cultural capital necessary for success in school. While many scholars would agree that schools promote and reward the knowledge and skills of the middle and upper classes, they counter the notions of cultural deficiency or disadvantage among Mexican Americans. Instead, they argue that these students come to school with a valuable and rich set of cultural and linguistic knowledge and skills. The following concepts and theoretical frameworks advance this perspective.

Community Cultural Wealth

Many scholars have developed frameworks that focus on the strengths Mexican Americans and other students of color bring to schools, as well as on how schools can best use those strengths for academic success. They argue that these students bring to school a wealth of capital that is most often unrecognized and unused by schools. Yosso (2005) has identified various forms of community cultural wealth that Mexican Americans offer, including aspirational, linguistic, familial, social, navigational, and

Figure 14. Forms of capital in community cultural wealth model. Source: Courtesy of Arturo Delgado Murillo.

resistant (see, e.g., Delgado Bernal, 1998, 2002; Faulstich Orellana, 2003; Gándara, 1982, 1995; Giroux, 1983; D. G. Solórzano & Yosso, 2000; Stanton-Salazar, 2001). These forms of community cultural wealth, each briefly discussed next, are not mutually exclusive or even static but may overlap and change over time to meet the needs of circumstances.

ASPIRATIONAL CAPITAL   Aspirational capital is the hope parents have for their children to succeed, despite societal obstacles. This form of capital includes the dreams or high aspirations parents have for their children to succeed in school, regardless of their own educational levels or socioeconomic living conditions. Aspirational capital can be transmitted through stories or consejos that parents, grandparents, or other elders tell children using their own life struggles as examples. Consejos are "spontaneous homilies designed to influence behaviors and attitudes" (Valdés, 1996, p. 125). Some parental consejos may include stories about their own or someone else's mistakes, a lack of opportunities they experienced, or how the child should follow the example of a respected role model or take advantage of new opportunities.

LINGUISTIC CAPITAL.   Linguistic capital involves the skills acquired by children who are bilingual or **bidialectical**. Linguistic capital can include a wealth of communication styles and skills or experiences, such as learning and telling stories (*cuentos*), oral histories, jokes, or proverbs (*dichos*).

Linguistic capital may require skills such as memorization, attention to detail, dramatic pauses, comedic timing, facial affect, vocal tone, volume, rhythm, and rhyme (Yosso, 2005). Also, because bilingual children often serve as translators or liaisons between their parents and external institutions such as schools, they develop the cognitive and social skills associated with those tasks.

FAMILIAL CAPITAL. Familial capital refers to cultural knowledge that comes from family or community, based on a shared history or experiences. This form of capital from family (which can include aunts, uncles, godparents, or other people defined as kin) and community includes emotional and moral support from their tight-knit network and a caring and trusting bond that supports educational or occupational pursuits.

SOCIAL CAPITAL. Social capital includes networks that provide emotional support, guidance, or resources for a particular path (discussed in more detail later). For example, a high-achieving peer group can provide guidance for choosing the appropriate high school courses for college entry. This can also include peers who provide each other with support or information on where to access a computer for homework, high school counselors or teachers who provide information on getting a scholarship for college, and mentors who provide knowledge about important criteria in selecting a college.

NAVIGATIONAL CAPITAL. Navigational capital provides knowledge about processes and institutions that were not set up with Mexican Americans in mind and, therefore, do not address their specific needs. Mexican American students who are the first in their family to go to college might be assisted by navigational capital on how to get into college, get into a certain class, see or ask the right questions of a counselor, delineate an informed college path, or get traditional and other forms of financial aid. Navigational capital can help Mexican American students, especially those with low income or whose parents have limited education, obtain information they might not normally have access to or be aware of, which can facilitate educational pursuits.

RESISTANT CAPITAL. Resistant capital refers to knowledge and skills used to oppose unequal treatment or conditions that create barriers. This can include attitudes or behaviors such as ways to persevere in the face of obstacles or understanding a context from an alternative perspective that provides insight to unequal conditions. In school, resistant capital may take the form of a student trusting his or her own academic record and taking an honors class even after an "easier" course was recommended, insisting on applying to a four-year university even after being told that community college might be a better first step exclusively due to cost, or starting an online petition or blog to protest and provide and receive information regarding a ban on Mexican American–related courses or books.

Funds of Knowledge

Funds of knowledge (a form of familial capital discussed earlier) views the culture that Mexican American students bring to school as valuable. This framework considers cultural knowledge important to allow students to succeed academically. Funds of knowledge is not a specific list of traits that are unchangeable over time or through specific social, economic, and political circumstances; on the contrary, they are variable and can be unique to specific contexts. Funds of knowledge "refers to those historically developed and accumulated strategies (skills, abilities, ideas, practices) or bodies of knowledge that are essential to a household's functioning and well-being" (González et al., 2005, pp. 91–92). In this framework, Mexican American students and other marginalized groups bring culturally and intellectually rich knowledge from home and the community. For example, Mexican American students may come to school with funds of knowledge about farming, mechanics, transborder trade, herbal medicine, child care, sales, home improvement, sewing, or a vast and diverse array of knowledge and skills specific to their households and communities and their changing needs. These funds of knowledge, however, are often unknown or unrecognized by schools, and therefore, Mexican American students are seen as lacking skills and knowledge considered valuable.

Using the funds of knowledge of Mexican American students in schools as a pedagogical resource is critical to their learning. Teachers are key players in learning what knowledge and skills students bring from home. Moreover, as some teachers learn about students' funds of knowledge, it helps them to "unlearn" viewing Mexican American students from a deficit perspective. Finally, teachers are able to develop curriculum that incorporates the funds of knowledge from Mexican American communities and use these to link to science, math, history, and other areas of study. Incorporating culturally relevant curriculum allows for continuity between home and school, validates the wealth of resources students bring with them from home, and empowers students and parents.

Social Capital and Social Networks

Social capital (one form of community cultural wealth discussed earlier) is another framework focusing on home and school support and resources to promote academic achievement. More specifically, "social capital refers to social relationships from which an individual is potentially able to derive institutional support that includes the delivery of knowledge-based resources, for example, guidance for college admission or job advancement" (Stanton-Salazar & Dornbusch, 1995, p. 119). In social capital theory relating to education, social networks (social ties or relationships) provide avenues for students to receive institutional support that can facilitate upward mobility and success in school. For some scholars of social capital theory, a main premise is that not all people in society have equal access to social networks that provide needed academic information and supports. Moreover, since American society is stratified and unequal based on power differences by race/ethnicity, social class, and gender, less privileged or marginalized groups are more likely excluded from critical social networks. Thus, Mexican American students, as a racial/ethnic group with a large working-class and poor population, are often excluded from important social networks that provide valuable knowledge and resources for educational success.

In the social capital framework, agents transmit resources and opportunities to students. Institutional agents can include school peers, teachers, and counselors but also middle-class family members and college-going community members (Stanton-Salazar, 1997). Social networks that support students in school can come in many forms, such as clubs, special programs (e.g., honors programs, Achievement Via Individual Determination), and institutional agents (e.g., teachers, counselors). The information and support Mexican American students receive in social networks include tutoring, mentoring, college resources for undocumented students, guidance on taking the appropriate courses for college admittance, information on the college application process, choosing a college, and career guidance, among many other resources and support. For Mexican American students, institutional agents in particular may be one of the few avenues for receiving the kinds of information necessary for academic and occupational mobility.

Students whose parents are unfamiliar with the American school system, were not provided college preparatory resources as students themselves, or did not attend college are especially dependent on schools for receiving knowledge and resources about successful high school and college progression and completion. If schools either do not provide this information or reserve it for a select group of students (e.g., honors students), this creates additional barriers for educational mobility, especially for working-class and poor students of color.

Transformative Pedagogies

Many pedagogical models challenge traditional models of teaching and learning and are believed to benefit socioeconomically disenfranchised, racial/ethnic, and female students, including Mexican Americans. In most traditional models of teaching, the following is assumed:

- knowledge is fixed,
- teachers are experts in the classroom,
- students do not have valuable knowledge to contribute to their learning,
- students' role is to learn passively (primarily through teacher lecture and student memorization), and
- knowledge considered legitimate is defined by the school.

In critical pedagogy (detailed shortly), this teaching model is referred to as "banking" education, whereby students are often seen as empty receptacles ready to be "filled" by knowledgeable teachers (Freire, 1970). Transformative pedagogical models challenge this traditional model of teaching. They view knowledge as developing continually and within social contexts, as made up of differing legitimate perspectives (not as a singular knowledge of the world), and as capable of changing as new information or evidence is uncovered. Also, teachers are viewed as both educators and learners and not exclusively as the "imparters" of knowledge. Moreover, students can generate knowledge, have important knowledge and experiences to contribute to their learning, and should be actively engaged in their learning by interacting with their peers and teachers.

Transformative pedagogical models consider the assumptions of the traditional model of teaching oppressive and, therefore, propose alternative models. Transformative pedagogies share two ideas: 1) There are dominant and subordinate power groups in society. Subordinate groups are disadvantaged in schools because their culture, language, and/or lived experiences are devalued and excluded from the classroom. 2) Transformative pedagogical models create a path for students from subordinate groups to become empowered and take action toward a democratic and nonoppressive society. The following discussion focuses on three transformative pedagogies and related theories that address educational issues affecting the academic achievement of Mexican Americans and other students of color.

Critical Pedagogy

Critical pedagogy is a teaching and learning framework based on the principles of critical theory. Therefore, critical pedagogy is concerned with power and inequality in schools and working toward democratic change. Darder, Baltodano, and Torres (2003) state,

> Critical pedagogy is fundamentally committed to the development and evolvement of a culture of schooling that supports the empowerment of culturally marginalized and economically disenfranchised students. By doing so, this pedagogical perspective seeks to help transform those classroom structures and practices that perpetuate undemocratic life. Of particular importance, then, is a critical analysis and investigation into the manner in which traditional theories and practices of schooling thwart or influence the development of a politically emancipatory and humanizing culture of participation, voice and social action within the classroom. (p. 11)

A goal of critical pedagogy, then, is to "unmask" or make visible the advantageous power relationship between dominant groups and schools, critiquing and challenging it by trying to make schools more democratic by giving disenfranchised groups, especially students, power.

Educational philosopher Paulo Freire is considered to be the most influential thinker in the development of critical pedagogy. Freire's popular concept of banking education is based on the ideas that schools devalue student knowledge and culture by not acknowledging them or connecting them to learning and that teachers are the only experts in the classroom. Thus, students are viewed as passive and lacking knowledge by being "depositories" of knowledge while teachers are viewed as all-knowledgeable and "depositors" of knowledge. In this traditional model of teaching (banking), students are thought to be learning by memorizing and repeating what the teacher presents, and teachers are thought to be teaching by presenting preapproved knowledge. In reality, this dynamic represents a lack of empowerment for both students and teachers because of the way learning and teaching are conceptualized. Critical pedagogy assumes that this dynamic upholds unequal and oppressive relations in school because it "negates education and knowledge as processes of inquiry" (Freire, 1970, p. 53).

To counteract this oppressive condition, critical pedagogy proposes that both teachers and students play an active role in changing the culture of schools so that it is inclusive and empowering. Teachers are charged with reflecting on, critiquing, and questioning traditional educational and teaching practices and transforming classroom conditions to create a liberatory environment. The classroom becomes a place where students are empowered by having their culture and the social realities of their lives respected and integrated and by actively participating and contributing to their learning through problem posing and dialogue. They are not merely objects in the classroom but empowered subjects. Students are also empowered by an analysis of school practices based on an understanding of their own marginalization and inferior position in schools. Students can resist oppressive power dynamics as they are unmasked through critique. Moreover, students develop a deepened awareness that their own life conditions have a historical and social context in a society with unequal power relations and that they can actively work to transform school and, then, society (referred to as conscientização or conscientization). The combined effect of reflection, interaction, and action or praxis is necessary to develop critical consciousness. Therefore, critical pedagogy seeks to change schools so that they do not support dominant groups exclusively but democratize relations of power so that all groups have input regarding the conditions (e.g., culture, curriculum, modes of assessment) of school.

Multicultural Education

Multicultural education assumes that race, ethnicity, culture, and social class are salient parts of U.S. society. However, school curriculum has not reflected the diversity of American society and has featured a primarily Anglo-centric orientation. Due to the exclusion of other groups, multicultural education seeks educational equity for students from diverse backgrounds such as those related to social class, gender, race, ethnicity, culture, and language. Nevertheless, there is not one specific way to put multicultural education into practice, and it can vary greatly. However, most leading multicultural education advocates argue that it must include antiracist, antisexist education that critiques oppressive institutions and practices in society and seeks to change them.

James Banks (1999), a leading proponent of multicultural education, states, "A key goal of multicultural education is to help individuals gain greater self-understanding by viewing themselves from the perspectives of other cultures. Multicultural education assumes that with acquaintance and understanding respect may follow" (p. 2). In addition to greater self-understanding and intergroup respect, another major goal of multicultural education includes providing students with cultural and ethnic alternatives to enrich them with the music, literature, values, lifestyles, and perspectives of a variety of groups. Moreover, Banks states that multicultural education is to provide "all students with the skills, attitudes, and knowledge needed to function within their ethnic culture, the mainstream culture, and within and across other ethnic cultures" (p. 2). Thus, multicultural education is intended for the benefit of all students living in a culturally diverse society, regardless of background, and for the benefit of a democratic society.

Advocates of multicultural education argue that the cultural and linguistic marginalization or exclusion of diverse groups from the curriculum and school culture has led to feelings of being different or not belonging or the need (or push) to change oneself to dominant cultural standards by students whose cultures and languages are inconsistent with school culture and norms. The dissonance felt by marginalized groups can lead to a disconnection with school and fewer opportunities for academic success. Hence, multicultural education is intended to bridge the gap between these groups and schools and to allow students to experience empowerment through knowledge and perspectives of self and others in the curriculum.

Nieto (2002) identifies the following seven characteristics of multicultural education as a form of empowerment:

- Multicultural education is antiracist education. This includes examining favoritism or privilege in all aspects of society and working to combat racism.
- Multicultural education is basic education. It is an indispensable part of a student's general education.
- Multicultural education is not only meant for specific groups but is important for all students, regardless of ethnicity, social class,

language, sexual orientation, religion, gender, race, or any other difference.

- Multicultural education is pervasive. It is infused in everything that happens at the school, including the school climate, physical environment, and curriculum and the relationships among the teachers, students, and community.

- Multicultural education is education for social justice. Schools should instill social justice by teaching students about active membership in a democracy and putting what they learn into action when faced with injustice in society.

- Multicultural education is a process. Education should emphasize continuous learning and asking critical questions. Sensitive and understanding relationships between teachers and students are also key.

- Multicultural education is critical pedagogy. A critical view of society, school, and knowledge is encouraged. Multiple perspectives are also important.

Although some may view multicultural education simply as "feel good" or appeasing education where students learn "only" about themselves and others, proponents argue that it is meant to address questions of stratification and inequity in society through power awareness, empowerment, and action.

Home-School Partnerships

One strand of research on improving the educational outcomes of Mexican American students focuses on the importance of home-school partnerships. Traditionally in American schools, the power dynamic is in the hands of schools. That is, schools direct what students learn, how they learn it, and when it should be learned. Students are expected to conform to the structure, values, and pace of the school environment. Much of the research on home-school partnerships contends that, while schools often espouse a philosophy of "partnering" with parents in the education of their children, the reality is that parents do not play a critical decision-making role in what takes place in schools. What traditional schools envision as parent involvement is often limited to helping children with homework, attending parent-teacher conferences and open houses, and supporting the school by volunteering or participating in parent organizations. These forms of parent involvement certainly are important, but they do not represent an equal partnership between parents and schools. In this traditional model of parent involvement, schools direct parent participation, and parents play a passive role. Many scholars who focus on Mexican Americans and parent involvement are critical of this model because it structures an unequal power dynamic. They propose changing power dynamics so that parents have meaningful power in their children's schools. Additionally, mutual understanding and respect need to be developed between schools and the communities they serve.

In the last few decades, research on home-school partnerships between Mexican American parents and schools has focused on learning about and respecting the knowledge, skills, and resources Mexican American families provide their children. Often, Mexican American families are invisible or not seen as valuable to student learning. As discussed previously, studies in this area often focus on identifying the community cultural wealth and funds of knowledge of Mexican American families and stress the importance of incorporating them in the classroom. Many scholars have identified a cultural gap or mismatch between immigrant Mexican American communities and schools. Often school solutions for addressing the mismatch come from a deficit perspective and involve interventions aimed at "fixing" Mexican American parents (e.g., classes on parenting). Scholars who have studied Mexican-origin communities recommend that instead, schools should focus on understanding and respecting the strengths of Mexican-origin families. Schools need to understand this group's values and linguistic competence, as opposed to trying to change families in ways that may undermine their values and childrearing practices. Addressing the cultural gap between Mexican American parents and schools is considered critical. Mexican American parents' expectations of teachers and schools, ways of interacting with schools, and help given their children are all areas of cultural misunderstandings that have led to negative stereotypes of these parents.

In Valdés's (1996) study of Mexican-origin immigrant families, she found differing expectations and misunderstandings between school personnel and immigrant parents. She found that immigrant family life focused on the well-being of the entire household (not just one child) and that the concept of *educación* (education) extended beyond education in an American academic sense to include raising a respectful, moral, and well-behaved child. *Respeto* (respect) in the family structure and community was of utmost importance in raising a child properly. While formal education was important to immigrant families, it did not define the success of a person in life. Instead, raising a child who exhibited educación and respeto was the critical foundation in assessing the success of a person.

While schools expect "standard" families to speak English and use middle-class norms in academic learning at home and interacting with the teacher, this often was viewed differently or as not possible by immigrant families. In Valdés's (1996) study, she notes,

> It did not occur to school personnel that parents might not know the appropriate ways to communicate with the teachers, that they might feel embarrassed about writing notes filled with errors, and that they might not even understand how to interpret their children's report cards. When children came to school without certain skills that the families, in good faith, believed the teachers should teach (e.g., the alphabet, the colors, the numbers), school personnel assumed parental indifference, troubled homes, and little interest in education. (p. 167)

Moreover, for some immigrant parents, schooling was viewed as the province and expertise of teachers and school personnel, not parents. For example, in another study on Latino immigrant families and schools, one parent commented,

> I didn't feel that I needed to know who my children's teachers were because I trusted that they knew what they were doing. I didn't know what my children needed because I didn't have much schooling in Mexico, so why should I question what they were doing in the classroom? I'm not the one that was educated to be a teacher. (Delgado-Gaitan, 2001, p. 28)

A lack of communication with the school could be viewed by the school as a parent's lack of concern for a child's education while, by examining the comment by the Latino parent just quoted, it might simply be deference to school authority and expertise.

Delgado-Gaitan (2004) advises that both Latino parents and schools need to reach out to each other. She proposes three important ways to increase parental involvement in Latino communities. First, connecting with Latino parents in a language they understand through teachers, other school personnel, and community liaisons is important for them to feel included in their children's education. Second, sharing information is critical and a two-way process. Educators should inform parents of what their child is doing in school and learn about the child's experience in the family. Finally, keeping parents involved is an ongoing process that needs constant assessment and revision. There is no single recipe for parental involvement, and thus, it should be tailored to specific communities and school districts.

There can be a gap between the expectations of immigrant and working-class Mexican American families and school personnel regarding parental involvement. Certainly both need to try to learn about and understand each other. However, it is clear that schools have the power to facilitate parental involvement and can dismiss parents who do not participate in ways considered appropriate as "not valuing" education. One important component of changing parent-school relations could be aided by schools recognizing and using the strengths of Mexican American families, creating avenues for parental input. Parents also need to recognize that they have a right and need to advocate on behalf of their children. Perhaps then parents and schools could truly work together and be considered mutually valuable partners supporting the academic success of Mexican American children.

Best Practices or Models for Urban Students and Students of Color

Substantial research attempting to explain low academic achievement (some research stemming from reproduction theory), especially for poor students and students of color, has focused specifically on unequal school conditions. This research has focused on inadequate funding of schools, inferior resources, school organization, ability grouping, curriculum tracking, low expectations, and less experienced or highly transient teachers at urban, impoverished, and racially segregated schools. This research attributes the poor achievement of Mexican American students to inferior school conditions. Chapter 2 discusses in more detail research that examines racial segregation and curriculum tracking as factors contributing to unequal school conditions for Mexican American students.

Research has also focused on the characteristics of schools that have had successful outcomes for students. Various practices or models have been proposed to best serve these students. Known as "best practices," the premise behind this research is identifying specific strategies or practices that enable schools to address many of the issues affecting urban and poor students and students of color, including Mexican American students. Some research has put the conditions of schooling into a political, economic, and social context with an understanding of power differences between various groups in society, while other research has not. That is, some research might view poor schooling conditions as part of larger social (including racial) and economic inequalities in American society, or through the lens of a critical view of the purpose of education (whose interests does education serve?), while other research does not.

School Characteristics

"Effective schools" is one area of research that focuses on identifying school characteristics correlated with high student achievement among low-income students and students of color. In this framework, the main premise is that by addressing the organizational weaknesses of low-income and minority-dominant schools, educational outcomes for students would be improved. Effective schools' research focuses on the school's ideology, organizational structure, and instructional practices (Brookover, 1985). Using this focus, researchers have identified five school characteristics that promote student achievement:

- high expectations for student achievement on the part of teachers and school staff
- strong instructional leadership on the part of the school principal and ·staff
- emphasis on mastery of basic skills
- frequent monitoring of student progress
- orderly and safe school environment (Edmonds, 1981)

Low-income and minority-dominant schools with these characteristics had more successful academic outcomes for students, and thus, the idea was that these could be replicated in similar schools for improved outcomes. One criticism of effective schools research is that it is too narrowly focused on fixing schools, as if schools in isolation were the problem. There is no focus on out-of-school factors, such as the causes of poor conditions in schools or even the conditions for low-income students and students of color in other arenas such as housing and the labor market.

School Characteristics and Culturally Responsive Pedagogy

Other research, similar in some ways to effective schools research, has examined the characteristics of high-performing schools, with a focus on Latino-dominant schools and an emphasis on characteristics that acknowledge the importance of culture and community. Scribner and Reyes (1999) identified four action dimensions found in high-performing learning communities for Latino students:

Action Dimension I. Community and family involvement are essential to the development of a high-performing learning community for Hispanic students.

Action Dimension II. High-performing learning communities for Hispanic students depend on leadership at all levels that supports collaborative governance that enables every student to succeed.

Action Dimension III. Culturally responsive pedagogy is required for students to succeed in a high-performing learning community for Hispanic students.

Action Dimension IV. Advocacy-oriented assessment that motivates the individual learning of the student is crucial to sustaining a high-performing learning community for Hispanic students. (p. 192)

This research expands the effective schools research by incorporating strategies that meet the needs of culturally and linguistically diverse students. These dimensions move beyond school characteristics and organization by recognizing the importance of family and community, a culturally responsive pedagogy, and an advocacy-oriented assessment. A culturally responsive pedagogy is one in which teachers believe in and verbalize students' ability to achieve; provide a caring environment where students are valuable resources; empower students by modes of learning that include innovation, discovery, and problem solving; engage in dialogue with students to make use of higher-order thinking skills; and use students' funds of knowledge in instructional practices. Advocacy-oriented assessment is primarily concerned with the progress of individual students and using a diverse array of assessment information that acknowledges students' cultural background, not exclusive dominance of high-stakes tests to assess students. The overarching focus of advocacy-oriented assessment is student learning, however, not for grade assignment or between-school comparisons, which are often tied to rewards and punishments.

School Structure and Culture

Researchers have also examined high academic achievement at low-income and minority-dominant schools by examining how the relationship between institutional structures and cultural forces affects educational outcomes. In this framework, school contexts promote positive or negative academic outcomes for students by influencing identity and peer culture. Conchas's (2006) study found three conditions that negatively affected the engagement of students of color with school: racial segregation in the school, divisions within racial groups, and differences in the institutional (school) support students receive. In this type of environment, school structures re-create societal racial separation and hierarchies, which promotes the idea that some racial groups are smarter than others or that only a small number of students of color are "smart" and, thus, deserving of a rigorous curriculum.

This area of research posits that racial identity and experience are not monolithic or static and, therefore, focuses on how school structures and practices influence positive racial and ethnic identities and peer cultures that promote success in school. School structures and cultures that promote racial integration and equal access to a rigorous academic area of study can influence academic success for students of color by promoting their student identities and a mutually supportive peer culture. For example, in Conchas's (2001) study of urban immigrant and native-born Latino students, he found that of three programs of study at a high school, the one that intentionally integrated various racial groups and students of differing academic achievement into its program had positive academic outcomes. This program promoted cultural awareness and student success and created a supportive (for some, family-like) learning community, benefiting Latinos' student engagement, sense of belonging, interracial group contact, peer relationships, and motivation to succeed in school and in a profession. Due to the structure and culture of this program, Latinos viewed themselves and other Latinos as academically oriented and successful.

Concluding Thoughts

School has often been assumed to be a neutral environment and a place that welcomes and accommodates the needs of all students and their families.

However, many scholars have concluded that schools are not neutral due to specific cultures, norms, and practices that can marginalize and disadvantage some students. These scholars have developed theories that examine how unequal power dynamics operate and perpetuate inequality in American society.

Other important theories have examined the cultural gap between Mexican American students and families and schools. When Mexican American families do not fit into normative school expectations, it is sometimes assumed that they lack concern for their children's education or are deficient in some way in promoting academic success. The scholarship examined in the chapter emphasized academic value in traits that emerge from Mexican American cultures, familial life, and experiences, even if they are not consistent with school culture and behaviors. Frameworks that redefine capital propose that Mexican American cultural capital should be acknowledged and integrated into the classroom. Likewise, transformative pedagogical frameworks bring culture into the classroom but also focus on empowering students and parents to make changes in school and society. Other research discussed emphasized the importance of home-school partnerships to empower parents and balance power in schools. Finally, this chapter examined models that focus on how organizational characteristics of schools and culture can support high achievement for Mexican American students.

Discussion Exercises

1. According to CRT and LatCrit theories, why is the ideology of American meritocracy problematic? How might this ideology affect people of color and poor families?

2. Develop a skit that integrates two forms of capital in the community cultural wealth framework. Can you think of any other forms of capital that students of color bring to school?

3. Why is integrating Mexican American funds of knowledge into the classroom important for Mexican American students?

4. Compare critical pedagogy to "banking" education. How might critical pedagogy improve the educational experiences of Mexican American youth?

5. What is the traditional relationship between parents and schools? How does this relationship work against low-income and immigrant parents? How

do you think relations between Mexican American parents and schools can be improved?

Suggested Readings

Banks, J. A., & Banks, C. A. M. (2001). *Handbook of research on multicultural education*. San Francisco: Jossey-Bass.

Darder, A., Baltodano, M., & Torres, R. D. (2009). *The critical pedagogy reader* (2nd ed.). New York: Routledge.

Delgado Bernal, D., Elenes, C. A., Godinez, F. E., & Villenas, S. (2006). *Chicana/ Latina education in everyday life: Feminista perpectives on pedagogy and epistemology*. Albany: State University of New York Press.

González, N., Moll, L. C., & Amanti, C. (2005). *Funds of knowledge: Theorizing practice in households, communities, and classrooms*. Mahwah, NJ: Lawrence Erlbaum.

Stanton-Salazar, R. D. (2001). *Manufacturing hope and despair: The school and kin support networks of U.S.-Mexican youth*. New York: Teachers College Press.

Valdés, G. (1996). *Con respeto: Bridging the distances between culturally diverse families and schools: An ethnographic portrait*. New York: Teachers College Press.

Yosso, T. J. (2006). *Critical race counterstories along the Chicana/o educational pipeline*. New York: Routledge.

Chapter 6

Not the Conclusion

Shifting the Paradigm

Many factors affect the academic achievement and attainment of Mexican American students. While Mexican American students have improved in the last few decades on many educational outcomes, as discussed throughout the book, there remains a persisting gap with their White peers and continuing concern in many areas, including standardized test scores, being pushed out of high school, and completing high school and college. As the Mexican American population in the United States and in public schools continues to grow, this group's academic achievement becomes increasingly important to the nation. In order for Mexican Americans to be full participants at all levels in the social, economic, and political arenas of society, unequal and oppressive school conditions must be addressed.

Change is needed on many levels in order to improve the educational attainment of Mexican American students. Inequalities in the larger society continue to permeate schools, leading to discrepancies in school conditions for wealthy and poor students. Large-scale structural inequalities need to be addressed (e.g., labor market discrimination) because they affect schools in many ways, including the perpetuation of racially and socioeconomically segregated schools and the distribution of school and community resources. Multiracial/ethnic alliances need to collaborate to confront unequal power dynamics in the social, political and economic arenas. Social policies that support poor and segregated families and communities must be strengthened. These include policies that support jobs, a living wage, affordable and quality housing, child care, and health and dental care, just to begin. Additionally, racism, sexism, classism, and other forms of oppression continue to affect how students are treated and what they have access to in school. One important step is immigration reform to create a path to citizenship for thousands of children who live in this country and many who only know this country. Much societal work still needs to take place in order to move toward empowering and democratic schools for all students.

Chapter 5 presented theoretical frameworks, pedagogies, and research that emphasized alternative models to traditional schooling for Mexican American students. These were labeled as critiques of power, redefined capital, transformational pedagogies and home-school partnerships (this conclusion focuses on these and continues using that labeling). While these certainly do not represent all of the approaches that need to be taken, they are an important component of changing schools to promote success for Mexican American students. How could these frameworks, pedagogies, and research be applied to understand, inform, and improve schooling for Mexican American students?

The challenges to traditional schooling these theoretical and pedagogical models propose go against deeply entrenched societal ideologies and norms about merit and achievement—that those who are successful in school worked harder or are more motivated than those who are considered average or not successful. Critiques of power theories propose that dominant ideologies of merit and achievement serve to mask societal inequalities. Thus, belief in ideologies based on innate racial, social class, and gender differences influences society's willingness to act and ability to see problems within the norms and practices of schools. It is easier to say that "[insert race or social class] are lazy students" or "[insert race or gender] are just naturally better at math" than to challenge the ideologies of merit and achievement. The idea of masked inequalities is evident when segregated schools are not seen as a major problem in American society even though schools are more racially segregated than they were before the *Brown* decision, which legally desegregated schools. Masked inequalities are evident when socioeconomic segregation in schools is considered inevitable because it is tied to where people "choose" to live, as if where people live is not tied to racial, social class, and gender inequalities. The inability to see problems is also evident when standardized testing and curriculum tracking, which divide students within schools by race and socioeconomic status, are not viewed as problematic because they are supported by the idea that only individual hard work and natural smarts get students high test scores or that students "choose" to be in the college-bound track. Thus, the taken-for-granted dominant ideology that the school system and the practices within it are colorblind, objective, and neutral allows inequality to continue with assumed legitimacy.

Theories that critique power also posit that those who benefit from an unequal system have an interest to maintain schools just as they are;

thus, normative, political, and economic barriers to equalizing schools are formidable. The role of power dynamics can be seen when privileged communities fight to maintain their advantages over poor communities. Even within the same schools, parents whose children receive more or better-quality resources than other children may view it as part of the competition to get into the best colleges and, thus, are not concerned with others receiving less but with how to maintain their edge. This was evident in attempts to detrack schools (discussed in chapter 2). Fierce opposition by powerful parents using dominant ideologies about merit and race and political maneuvering derailed these attempts, with parents claiming that their own children would be disadvantaged with detracking. No consideration was given to the reality that maintaining curriculum tracking as is, thus, maintaining racial and social class divisions, had been and would continue disadvantaging other people's children.

This fight to maintain privilege in schools can also be seen in the normative position of schools to view English learners as deficient for needing to learn English as opposed to advantaged for having the potential to develop bilingually and biculturally. Instead, monolingual English speakers are seen as advantaged in school despite an increasingly global world that requires multilingual and multicultural citizens and workers. Additionally, despite research that supports the cognitive advantages of bilingualism, most schools do not provide the opportunity for advanced and rigorous classes (e.g., advanced placement) for English learners. These perspectives and practices aid in maintaining unequal power in education and society. Thus, the challenge of changing the school system is not an easy one; multiple forms and levels of power must be confronted in schools and in the larger society.

Certainly, unmasking power as called for by critiques of power theories does not happen suddenly or at the will of marginalized groups or their allies. Changes in society have always taken time as society is influenced by external pressures and communities working together toward unmasking social, political, and economic power dynamics and challenging normative ideologies that uphold inequalities and silence critique. Communities comprise the human agency, evident in the civil rights and Chicano movements, that critiques of power considers central to change. As discussed in chapter 1, the numerous desegregation cases brought forth by Mexican Americans in the twentieth century are also examples of human agency. Most recently, this has been exemplified by Dreamers—youth who are fighting back against the dehumanizing effects of living in a society that wants only to define people as legal or illegal, as if nothing else matters. They and their allies have been fighting for a path to citizenship and educational rights. More importantly, they have been fighting for their dignity as human beings and the recognition that we are all the same. Their individual and community actions—organizing, educational forums, protests—have reached and influenced national politics. This is how power is unmasked and social change takes place.

In order to change schools, a paradigm shift is necessary. Schools would not reify socially constructed differences (e.g., who is smart and who is not) but view all students as capable of learning and as contributors to the generation and development of knowledge. Standardized tests would no longer be valid or useful for sorting students due to the recognition that scores are influenced by cultural, socioeconomic, and language differences. Additionally, student intellectual capabilities would be viewed as multifaceted and developing. The democratic power relations called for by transformative pedagogies would entail elimination of the hierarchal relations of superiority and inferiority at the heart of curriculum tracking. Higher-order thinking skills, including critical and analytic thinking and problem solving, would not be taught exclusively to high-track students but developed in all students because all would be viewed as possessing and capable of developing these skills and more. Independent and diverse thinking would be encouraged in schools.

Applying theories that redefine capital and the transformational pedagogies in schools would challenge the notion of a singular body of knowledge that is valuable and legitimate. These frameworks challenge this notion by integrating the knowledge, skills, and experiences of Mexican American students and their communities in school for teaching and learning. To be clear, there is no one way to apply or enact these frameworks because Mexican American students are diverse and live in a variety of communities. Nevertheless, schools would serve to develop those capabilities from Mexican American students' homes and communities and learn from them. Integrating the culture and lives of Mexican Americans students and parents would be part of a school paradigm shift. Alternative and diverse methods of assessment would be developed that incorporate and validate students' backgrounds and varied modes of learning. These new methods of assessment would be used to identify areas in need of development and not used as defining tools to label students as smart or low ability. Thus, the purpose and mode of testing would be changed. These changes are consistent with the goal of changing school structures and practices to promote social justice and democracy.

Additionally, schools would cultivate the various forms of capital that Mexican American students and their families bring. For example, if students assist their parents in a business, they may have knowledge of recordkeeping or competitive pricing that could be connected to math lessons. Understanding photosynthesis or Mendel's cross-pollination theory would be much more meaningful if plants that students have in their own or a family member's home are integrated. For example, the many colors of roses in a community may be useful examples for studying cross-pollination. Certainly, an analysis of tamales (and sister foods such as *nacatamales* and *hallacas*) throughout the Americas could tie history, agriculture, geography, globalism, politics, and culture into a cross-disciplinary classroom project.

By applying frameworks that redefine capital and transformational pedagogies, aspirational and familial capital would be assumed for Mexican American students. Mexican American parental support for school would be assumed as opposed to thought of as needing to be instilled in them. This would be the basis for a new home-school relationship. Additionally, understanding how parents define their involvement would be important for addressing school deficiencies. Acknowledging and working with the ways parents are involved would be cultivated and expanded. The involvement schools desire would be changed to integrate the strengths of parents. For example, parental contribution to school through donation of their home or work skills might be more beneficial than wrapping paper fund-raisers. Additionally, in schools with Spanish-speaking parents, all newsletters and communication would be translated to Spanish. This is essential for not cutting off these parents from school information and activities.

As discussed in chapter 2, Mexican Americans predominantly attend segregated schools. While integrating Mexican American capital will not address unequal and inferior resources at racially and socioeconomically segregated schools, it could provide a foundation for student and community empowerment for collaboration and advocacy. Additionally, by implementing theories that redefine capital and transformational pedagogies, segregated schools could cultivate resistant capital (that originates from family or community) if students are provided the tools and active learning opportunities to study the needs of their own school and community. This could further develop the critical consciousness that critiques of power and transformative pedagogies propose leads students to advocate for change. Mexican American students could be provided with opportunities to discuss, study, and actively work on issues affecting their own communities with fellow students and community members. Their research would generate new knowledge to inform old knowledge and provide additional perspectives. This would also serve to democratize power relations in schools because students would be valuable and integral contributors to their own and their classmates' and teachers' learning. Thus, learning would have social value and meaning to students.

Segregated and nonsegregated schools alike could also cultivate social networks and navigational capital for students by institutionalizing organizations and forums for disseminating information and collaborating. For example, programs such as Achievement Via Individual Determination (AVID), which supports college readiness by providing academic and social support, could be expanded to all students and renamed Achievement Via Mutual Support (this would reject any implication that students who do not go to college are simply not determined enough and acknowledge the institutional support that the program provides). The institutional and peer support of AVID provide the academic knowledge, resources, experiences, contacts, and encouragement to attend higher education. Cultivating students' leadership and advocacy skills could be added to equip students to take active roles in their communities and the larger society. Additionally, the program could integrate parent knowledge by highlighting the strengths developed through life's hardships and successes, providing strategic examples for students to model in pursuing higher education.

Shifting the paradigm of schools can empower students, enrich the curriculum, and connect home and school lives. Transformative pedagogies could be used to create a climate and practice in schools that welcomes and values all languages and cultures. For example, if Mexican American students' linguistic and familial capital is integrated into the classroom, students will feel valued and a sense of ownership to class activities. Mexican American students would be learners and teachers; likewise, teachers would take on both roles as well. The curriculum would be expanded to allow for cross-language or cross-dialect comparison and discussion. An analysis of Spanglish could provide Spanglish speakers the opportunity to provide examples of its syntax, which could be followed by class analysis and discussion. Thus, the inclusion and valuation of languages other than English and dialects of English (discussed in chapters 3 and 5) would be a school's practice and included in its culture. This would also support the democratization of power that transformative pedagogies advocate by not allowing non–English or non–standard English speakers to feel inferior in schools.

The integration of linguistic and familial capital would allow for a sense of wholeness as opposed to a cultural separation between the spheres of school and home. Many Mexican American students consider this separation normal because they have experienced it most of their school lives and may not even be aware of it until an element of one sphere crosses into the other. (For example, when I used the Spanish word *chancla* [sandal] in a college classroom, some students who understood Spanish were surprised and laughed that a familiar word from their home world crossed into their school world.) A sense of wholeness and belonging is why Chicana and Chicano studies programs (such as the one recently banned in Arizona) are so critical for K–12 and higher education. Integration of school and home allows a sense of connection to be normalized for Mexican American students. The cultural gap between Mexican American families and schools (identified in the research on home-school partnerships) would be addressed because cultural, linguistic, and familial capital would overlap both spheres. The hybridity and intersectionality (e.g., bidialecticalism, biculturalism) identified by critiques of power would be fully embraced and used to inform the curriculum and culture of schools. This would allow students to voice perspectives and insights not typically heard in school. Thus, they and their experiences would be centered in the classroom.

Change in society is necessary to address power inequalities embedded at many levels. From large-scale societal, political, and economic levels to small-scale daily interactions in the classroom, there must be a paradigm shift that respects and empowers all members of society.

Policy Recommendations

Researchers have developed policy recommendations to address continuing educational concerns for Mexican American students. Some policy recommendations have already been presented in previous chapters. Chapter

2 discussed specific recommendations to address the issues of increasing segregation and the overreliance and bias of educational testing. Policy recommendations for equalizing the learning conditions of English learners and linguistic minorities were presented in Chapter 3. Chapter 4 included recommendations for increasing community college transfers, where a large proportion of Mexican American students begin college, to four-year universities.

Yosso and Solórzano (2006) make recommendations focusing on many of the critical transition points discussed throughout the text, including preparing Mexican American K–12 students for college, community college students for transfer, and university undergraduate students for graduate school. Their recommendations are meant to address "leaks" in the educational pipeline and better prepare Mexican American students for educational mobility. They propose first to increase access to academic enrichment at K–12 levels (GATE, honors, AP, magnet) and, second, make basic college entrance requirements the "default" curriculum accessible to all high school students. These recommendations would address the underrepresentation of Mexican American students in programs with rigorous curriculum such as honors programs. This would assure access to the skills necessary for college-level work and the capital needed to understand and navigate the college experience. This is especially critical for potential first-generation college students. Third, decrease the overreliance on high-stakes, inappropriate testing and assessment. Mexican American students would not be excluded from rigorous curriculum programs or prohibited from graduating based on the results of single standardized tests. Additionally, linguistic minorities and English learners would not be assessed using tests created for English-only students but tests specifically for them.

Fourth, train bilingual, multicultural educators to challenge cultural deficit thinking and to acknowledge the cultural wealth of Chicana/o students. This recommendation supports an assets view of Chicana/o students that would recognize its value and center their cultural and linguistic resources in the curriculum and classroom environment. It also calls for training bilingual and multilingual teachers, a needed resource for multilingual students. Fifth, reach out to parents as educational partners. Parental involvement and input is essential for effective two-way communication, dispelling misunderstandings, and democratizing power relations between Mexican American parents and schools. Sixth, prioritize the transfer function as the central mission of community colleges. Recognizing the large proportion of community college students who never make the transition to a four-year university, this recommendation would focus on creating institutional and cultural supports such as timely advising, clear transfer information, and aid for family and work obligations.

Changes to educational policies and practices, such as those recommended by Yosso and Solórzano, are focused on ensuring school success for Mexican American students. As stated in the introduction to this text, Mexican American education has been characterized as "school failure" due to their low achievement. That low achievement is in no way a reflection of students' desire for education, the hard work and concern students put into their schoolwork, and the lengths parents will go to secure a quality education for their children. Nevertheless, the dominant ideologies and unequal school conditions discussed in this text continue to affect Mexican Americans' educational experiences and opportunities. Thus, their success, and the success of all students, is essential for a just American society.

GLOSSARY

amalgamation   The mixing or blending of different elements, races, or societies.

assimilation   The act or process of incorporating or absorbing; to bring into conformity with the customs and attitudes of a group, nation, or the like.

bidialectical   The ability to speak in two provincial or socially distinct varieties of a language.

Chicano movement   A political movement prominent during the 1960s and early 1970s in which large numbers of Mexican Americans advocated and actively worked toward equal treatment with other U.S. citizens.

class action   A lawsuit brought by a representative member or members of a large group on behalf of all members of the group.

cognitive   Of or pertaining to the mental processes of perception, memory, judgment, and reasoning, as contrasted with emotional and volitional processes.

concentrated poverty   May refer to the state of communities (or schools) in which high proportions of the population live in poverty.

cultural bias   Systemic discrimination against a racial/ethnic group.

cultural capital   The worth or value assigned to a social group's characteristics, including language, customs, and knowledge.

deculturalization   The process of removing a people's culture and replacing it with a new culture.

defendant   The party defending or denying; the party against whom relief or recovery is sought in an action or suit, or the accused in a criminal case.

de jure segregation   Separation directly mandated or intended by law.

desegregation   The process of ending separation of groups; to open (a school or workplace, for example) to members of all races or ethnic groups, especially by force of law.

detracking   Reducing or eliminating the levels of low-rigor curriculum tracks in schools due to the negative impact of these groupings on low-track students.

discourse   Dominant social messages or official master narratives.

double segregation Simultaneous separation or isolation by two characteristics, including race, poverty, or language.

English learners (ELs) Refers to students whose native language is not English and who are in the process of acquiring English.

Equal Protection Clause A provision in the Fourteenth Amendment of the U.S. Constitution that prohibits a state from denying to any person within its jurisdiction the equal protection of the laws.

gerrymander To manipulate geographic boundaries so as to give unfair advantage to one party in elections; may also apply to the manipulation of school district boundaries to keep schools racially exclusive.

high-stakes testing Achievement examinations in which the results have important life consequences for education (e.g., graduation) and career (e.g., teacher credential).

hypersegregation Extreme levels of spatial separation in domains such as schools or residential areas.

human agency Refers to the capacity of people to act independently and to make their own free choices.

ideology A system of beliefs and principles that presents an organized explanation of and justification for a person's or group's outlooks and behavior.

institutionalized Practices incorporated into a highly formalized system such as the political, economic, and educational systems.

linguistic minority In the United States, refers to students who come from households where a language other than English is spoken.

microaggressions Subtle but commonplace slights, insults, and indignities—whether intentional or unintentional—that communicate humiliating messages to a particular person or group.

monolingual A person with the ability to speak only one language.

National Assessment of Educational Progress A U.S. national assessment of student performance and educational achievement in a variety of subjects in elementary and secondary school.

normative A social group's standard of required or expected behavior.

overrepresented   When the proportion of a group in a sample is disproportionately larger than the proportion of that group in the general population.

plaintiff   The party who brings an action; the party who complains or sues in a civil action.

postbaccalaureate   Subsequent and in addition to the baccalaureate, or bachelor's, degree.

racialization   Refers to a process of assigning racial meaning (e.g., labels, stereotypes) to a previously racially unclassified relationship, social practice, or group.

resegregation   When segregation reoccurs.

second-generation segregation   Within-school segregation; the consequence of separating students in an integrated school that results in racial resegregation within the school (e.g., curriculum tracking).

socially constructed   A concept or practice that is the construct (or artifact) of a particular group.

standardized test   A test that is administered and scored in a consistent manner.

stratified   To be arranged or classified by status; division of a society into levels based on societal markers such as occupational or socioeconomic status.

subtractive bilingualism   A process in which students lose their first language while learning a second language.

theoretical framework   A group of general propositions and concepts used to explain or understand phenomena such as social inequality.

underrepresented   Insufficiently or inadequately represented; when the proportion of a group in a sample is disproportionately smaller than the proportion of that group in the general population.

undocumented   Refers to immigrants who reside in the United States but do not have the appropriate legal documents to do so.

xenophobia   Fear or hatred of foreigners or strangers.

BIBLIOGRAPHY

Abrego, L. (2008). Legitimacy, social identity, and the mobilization of law: The effects of assembly bill 540 on undocumented students in California. *Law and Social Inquiry, 33* (3), 709–34.

Achor, S., & Morales, A. (1990). Chicanas holding doctoral degrees: Social reproduction and cultural ecological approaches. *Anthropology and Education Quarterly, 21* (33), 269–87.

Acuña, R. (1972). *Occupied America: The Chicano's struggle toward liberation.* San Francisco: Canfield Press.

Alanis, J. (2010). *The Harrison High School walkouts of 1968: Struggle for equal schools and Chicanismo in Chicago.* Unpublished doctoral dissertation, University of Illinois at Urbana–Champaign.

Anzaldua, G. (1987). *Borderlands/la frontera: The new mestiza.* San Francisco: Aunt Lute Books.

Arredondo, G. F. (2003). *Chicana feminisms: A critical reader.* Durham, NC: Duke University Press.

Artiles, A. J., Waitoller, F. R., & Neal, R. (2011). Grappling with the intersection of language and ability differences. In R. R. Valencia (Ed.), *Chicano school failure and success: Past, present and future* (3rd ed., pp. 213–34). New York and London: Routledge.

Aud, S., Fox, M., & KewalRamani, A. (2010). *Status and trends in the education of racial and ethnic groups* (NCES 2010–015). Washington, DC: National Center for Education Statistics.

Aud, S., Hussar, W., Johnson, F., Kena, G., Roth, E., Manning, E., et al. (2012). *The condition of education 2012* (NCES 2012–045). Washington, DC: National Center for Education Statistics.

Aud, S., Hussar, W., Kena, G., Bianco, K., Frohlich, L., Kemp, et al. (2011). *The condition of education 2011* (NCES 2011–033). Washington, DC: National Center for Education Statistics.

Aud, S., Hussar, W., Planty, M., Snyder, T., & Bianco, K. (2010). *The condition of education 2010* (NCES 2010–028). Washington, DC: National Center for Education Statistics.

Auerbach, S. (2002). Why do they give the good classes to some and not to others? Latino parent narratives of struggle in a college access program. *Teachers College Record, 104* (7), 1369–92.

Baker, S., & Hakuta, K. (1997). *Bilingual education and Latino civil rights.* Paper presented at the Symposium on the Latino Civil Rights Crisis, UCLA Civil Rights Project and Thomas Rivera Policy Institute.

Ballón, E. G. (1999). *Math curriculum tracking and educational outcomes.* Unpublished doctoral dissertation, University of California, Los Angeles.

Ballón, E. G. (2008). Racial differences in high school math track assignment. *Journal of Latinos and Education, 7* (4), 272–87.

Banks, J. A. (1999). *An introduction to multicultural education* (2nd ed.). Boston: Allyn and Bacon.

Barrera, M. (1979). *Race and class in the Southwest: A theory of racial inequality.* South Bend, IN: University of Notre Dame Press.

Bell, D. (1992). Faces at the bottom of the well: The permanence of racism. New York: Basic Books.

Bell, D. (1995). Who's afraid of critical race theory? *University of Illinois Law Review, 4,* 893–910.

Bourdieu, P., & Passeron, J. C. (1977). *Reproduction in education, society and culture.* Beverly Hills, CA: Sage.

Bowles, S., & Gintis, H. (1976). *Schooling in capitalist America: Educational reform and the contradictions of economic life.* New York: Basic Books.

Braddock, J. H., & Dawkins, M. P. (1993). Ability grouping, aspirations, and attainments: Evidence from the National Educational Longitudinal Study of 1988. *Journal of Negro Education, 62* (3), 1–13.

Brookover, W. B. (1985). Can we make schools effective for minority students? *Journal of Negro Education, 54,* 257–68.

Callahan, R. M. (2013). *The English learner dropout dilemma: Multiple risks and multiple resources* (California Dropout Research Project Report #19). Santa Barbara, CA: Gervitz Graduate School of Education, UC.

Center on Education Policy. (2007). *State high school exit exams: Working to raise test scores.* Washington, DC: Center on Education Policy.

Chacon, J. M. (2008). Race as a diagnostic tool: Latinas/os and higher education in California, post-209. *California Law Review, 96* (5), 1215–57.

Charleston, L. V. J. (2009). The dilemma of higher education reform in a post-affirmative action society: A review of anti-affirmative action legislation to inform policy modification. *Annuals of the Next Generation, 2* (1), 10–26.

Chávez, C. (2007). *Five generations of a Mexican American family in Los Angeles.* Lanham, MD: Rowman and Littlefield.

Chavez, L. (2008). *Untapped potential: Latinos and California community colleges* (Policy Reports and Research Briefs). Berkeley: University of California, Center for Latino Policy Research.

Chávez-Reyes, C. (2010). "Starting at the top": Identifying and understanding later generation Chicano students in schools. *Journal of Latinos and Education, 9* (1), 22–40.

College Board. (2009). *SAT data: Tables & related items* (SAT Data and Reports). New York: The College Board.

Conchas, G. Q. (2001). Structuring failure and success: Understanding the variability in Latino school engagement. *Harvard Educational Review, 71* (3), 475–504.

Conchas, G. Q. (2006). *The color of success: Race and high-achieving urban youth.* New York: Teachers College Press.

Covarrubias, A. (2011). Quantitative intersectionality: A critical race analysis of the Chicana/o educational pipeline. *Journal of Latinos and Education, 10* (2), 86–105.

Covarrubias, A., & Lara, A. (2014). The undocumented migrant educational pipeline: The influence of citizenship status on educational attainment for people of Mexican origin. *Urban Education, 49* (1), 75–110.

Crawford, J. (2000). Language politics in the United States: The paradox of bilingual education. In C. Ovando & P. McLaren (Eds.), *The politics of multicultural and bilingual education: Students and teachers caught in the crossfire* (pp. 106–25). Boston: McGraw-Hill.

Crawford, J. (2008). *Advocating for English learners: Selected essays.* Clevedon, UK: Multilingual Matters.

Crenshaw, K., Gotanda, N., Peller, G., & Thomas, K. (Eds). (1995). *Critical race theory: The key writings that formed the movement.* New York: The New Press.

Cúadraz, G. H. (1996). Experiences of multiple marginality: A case study of Chicana "scholarship women." In C. Turner, M. Garcia, A. Nora, & L. Rendon (Eds.), *Racial & ethnic diversity in higher education—ASHE reader* (pp. 210–22). Boston: Pearson.

Cummins, J. (1979). Linguistic interdependence and the educational development of bilingual children. *Review of Educational Research, 49* (2), 222–51.

Cummins, J. (1989). *Empowering minority students.* Ontario, CA: California Association for Bilingual Education.

Darder, A., Baltodano, M., & Torres, R. D. (2003). Critical pedagogy: An introduction. In A. Darder, M. Baltodano, & R. D. Torres (Eds.), *The critical pedagogy reader* (1st ed., pp. 1–21). New York: Routledge Falmer.

De León, A. (1974). Blowout 1910 style: A Chicano school boycott in West Texas. *Texana, 12,* 124–40.

De León, A. (1982). *The Tejano community, 1836–1900.* Albuquerque: University of New Mexico Press.

Delgado, R. (Ed.). (1995). *Critical race theory: The cutting edge.* Philadelphia: Temple University Press.

Delgado Bernal, D. (1998). Grassroots leadership reconceptualized: Chicana oral histories and the 1968 East Los Angeles school blowouts. *Frontiers: A Journal of Women Studies, 19* (2), 113–42.

Delgado Bernal, D. (2000). Historical struggles for educational equity: Setting the context for Chicana/o schooling today. In C. Tejeda, C. Martinez, & Z. Leonardo (Eds.), *Charting new terrains of Chicana(o)/Latina(o) education* (pp. 67–90). Cresskill, NJ: Hampton Press.

Delgado Bernal, D. (2002). Critical race theory, LatCrit theory and critical raced-gendered epistemologies: Recognizing students of color as holders and creators of knowledge. *Qualitative Inquiry, 8* (1), 105–26.

Delgado Bernal, D. (2006). Learning and living pedagogies of the home: The mestiza consciousness of Chicana students. In D. Delgado Bernal, C. A. Elenes, F. E. Godinez, & S. Villenas (Eds.), *Chicana/Latina education in everyday life: Feminista perspectives on pedagogy and epistemology* (pp. 113–32). Albany: State University of New York Press.

Delgado-Gaitan, C. (2001). *The power of community: Mobilizing for family and schooling*. Lanham, MD: Rowman and Littlefield.

Delgado-Gaitan, C. (2004). *Involving Latino families in schools: Raising student achievement through home-school partnerships*. Thousand Oaks, CA: Corwin.

Delpit, L. (1995). *Other people's children: Cultural conflict in the classroom*. New York: New Press.

Donato, R. (1997). *The other struggle for equal schools: Mexican Americans during the civil rights era*. Albany: State University of New York Press.

Donato, R. (2007). *Mexicans and Hispanos: In Colorado schools and communities, 1920–1960*. Albany: State University of New York Press.

Donato, R., & Hanson, J. S. (2012). Legally white, socially "Mexican": The politics of de jure and de facto school segregation in the American Southwest. *Harvard Educational Review, 82* (2), 202–25.

Edmonds, R. (1981). *The characteristics of effective schools: Research and implementation*. Unpublished manuscript, Michigan State University.

English Plus movement: Statement of purpose & core beliefs. (1987). Retrieved January 19, 2011, from http://www.massenglishplus.org/mep/engplus.html.

Ennis, S. R., Ríos-Vargas, M., & Albert, N. G. (2011). *The Hispanic population: 2010* (C2010BR-04). Washington, DC: U.S. Census Bureau.

Faulstich Orellana, M. (2003). *In other words: Learning from bilingual kids' translating and interpreting experiences*. Evanston, IL: School of Education and Social Policy, Northwestern University.

Freeman, R. (2004). Reviewing the research on language education programs. In O. Garcia & C. Baker (Eds.), *Bilingual education: An introductory reader*. Clevedon, UK: Multilingual Matters.

Freire, P. (1970). *Pedagogy of the oppressed*. New York: Continuum.

Fry, R. (2002). *Latinos in higher education: Many enroll, too few graduate*. Washington, DC: Pew Hispanic Center.

Fry, R. (2005). *Recent changes in the entry of Hispanic and white youth into college*. Washington, DC: Pew Hispanic Center.

Fry, R. (2007). *How far behind in math and reading are English language learners?* Washington, DC: Pew Hispanic Center.

Fry, R., & Taylor, P. (2013). *Hispanic high school graduates pass whites in rate of college enrollment*. Washington, DC: Pew Hispanic Center.

Gamoran, A. (1987). The stratification of high school learning opportunities. *Sociology of Education, 60*, 135–55.

Gamoran, A., & Mare, R. D. (1989). Secondary school tracking and educational inequality: Compensation, reinforcement or neutrality? *American Journal of Sociology, 94,* 1146–83.

Gándara, P. (1982). Passing through the eye of the needle: High-achieving Chicanas. *Hispanic Journal of Behavioral Sciences, 4,* 167–79.

Gándara, P. (1995). *Over the ivy walls: The educational mobility of low-income Chicanos.* Albany: State University of New York Press.

Gándara, P. (1999a). *Subtractive schooling: U.S.-Mexican youth and the politics of caring.* Albany: State University of New York Press.

Gándara, P. (1999b). Staying in the race: The challenge for Chicanos/as in higher education. In J. F. Moreno (Ed.), *The elusive quest for equality: 150 years of Chicano/Chicana education* (2nd ed., pp. 169–96). Cambridge, MA: Harvard Educational Review.

Gándara, P. (2005). Addressing educational inequities for Latino students: The politics of "forgetting." *Journal of Hispanic Higher Education, 4* (3), 295–313.

Gándara, P. (2009). Progress and stagnation: 25 years of Hispanic achievement. *Diverse Issues in Higher Education, 26* (9), 2.

Gándara, P., & Hopkins, M. (2010). The changing linguistic landscape of the United States. In P. Gándara, & P. Hopkins (Eds.), *Forbidden language: English learners and restrictive language policies* (pp. 7–19). New York: Teachers College Press.

Gándara, P., Maxwell-Jolly, J., & Rumberger, R. (2008). Resource needs for English learners: Getting down to policy recommendations. Berkeley: University of California Linguistic Minority Research Institute.

Gándara, P., & Rumberger, R. (2002). *The inequitable treatment of English learners in California's public schools. Williams Watch Series: Investigating the Claims of Williams v. State of California.* Los Angeles: UCLA Institute for Democracy, Education & Access.

Gándara, P., & Rumberger, R. (2006). Resource needs for California's English learners. Santa Barbara: UC Linguistic Minority Research Institute.

Gándara, P., Rumberger, R., Maxwell-Jolly, J., & Callahan, R. (2003). English learners in California schools: Unequal resources, unequal outcomes. *Education Policy Analysis Archives, 11* (36), 1–54.

García, E. E., & Wiese, A. M. (2002). Language, public policy, and schooling: A focus on Chicano English language learners. In R. Valencia (Ed.), *Chicano school failure and success: Past, present and future* (2nd ed., pp. 149–69). London: RoutlegeFalmer.

Garcia, O., & Baker, C. (2007). *Bilingual education: An introductory reader.* Clevedon, UK: Multilingual Matters.

Gibson, C., & Jung, K. (2002). *Historical census statistics on population totals by race, 1790 to 1990, and by Hispanic origin, 1970 to 1990, for the United States, regions, divisions, and states* (Working Paper Series No. 56). Washington, DC: U.S. Census Bureau.

Giroux, H. (1983). Theories of reproduction and resistance in the new sociology of education: A critical analysis. *Harvard Educational Review, 55,* 257–93.

Gomez, L. E. (2007). *Manifest destinies: The making of the Mexican American race.* Albany: New York University Press.

Gonzalez, G. G. (1990). *Chicano education in the era of segregation.* Philadelphia: Balch Institute Press.

Gonzalez, G. G. (1999). Segregation and the education of Mexican children. In J. F. Moreno (Ed.), *The elusive quest for equality: 150 years of Chicano/Chicana education* (2nd ed., pp. 53–76). Cambridge, MA: Harvard Educational Review.

Gonzalez, G. G. (2000). The ideology and practice of empire: The U.S., Mexico, and the education of Mexican immigrants. *Cultural Logic: An Electronic Journal of Marxist Theory and Practice, 4* (1).

González, N., Moll, L. C., Tenery, M. F., Rivera, A., Rendon, P., Gonzales, R., et al. (2005). Funds of knowledge for teaching in Latino households. In N. González, L. C. Moll, & C. Amanti (Eds.), *Funds of knowledge: Theorizing practices in households, communities, and classrooms* (pp. 89–111). Mahwah, NJ: Lawrence Erlbaum.

Gordon, M. M. (1964). *Assimilation in American life: The role of race, religion, and national origins.* New York: Oxford University Press.

Gutiérrez, J. A. (2005). *We won't back down: Severita Lara's rise from student leader to mayor.* Houston, TX: Arte Público Press/Piñata Books.

Hakuta, K. (1986). *Mirror of language: The debate on bilingualism.* New York: Basic Books.

Hakuta, K., Butler, Y. G., & Witt, D. (2000). *How long does it take English learners to attain proficiency?* Santa Barbara: UC Linguistic Minority Research Institute.

Herrnstein, R. J., & Murray, C. (1994). *The bell curve: Intelligence and class structure in American life.* New York: Free Press.

Horn, L., Nevill, S., & Griffith, J. (2006). *Profile of undergraduates in U.S. postsecondary education institutions: 2003–04 with a special analysis of community college students* (NCES 2006–184). Washington, DC: National Center for Education Statistics.

Human Resources Research Organization. (2013). *Independent evaluation of the California High School Exit Examination: 2013 evaluation. Report prepared for California Department of Education.* Alexandria, VA.

Hurtado, S., Saenz, V. B., Santos, J. L., & Cabrera, A. L. (2008). Advancing in higher education: A portrait of Latina/o college freshman at four-year institutions, 1975–2006. Los Angeles: University of California, Higher Education Research Institute.

Kao, G., & Tienda, M. (1995). Optimism and achievement: The educational performance of immigrant youth. *Social Science Quarterly, 76* (1), 1–19.

Kornhaber, M. L., & Orfield, G. (2001). High-stakes testing policies: Examining their assumptions and consequences. In M. L. Kornhaber & G. Orfield (Eds.), *Raising standards or raising barriers? Inequality and high stakes testing in public education* (pp. 1–18). New York: Century Foundation Press.

Krashen, S. D. (1996). *Under attack: The case against bilingual education*. Culver City, CA: Language Education Associates.

Krashen, S. D. (1999). *Condemned without a trial: Bogus arguments against bilingual education*. Portsmouth, NH: Heinemann.

Krashen, S. D., Tse, L., & McQuillan, J. (Eds.). (1998). *Heritage language development*. Culver City, CA: Language Education Associates.

Maceda, J. (1997). English only: The tongue-tying of America. In A. Darder, R. D. Torres, & H. Gutierrez (Eds.), *Latinos and education: A critical reader* (pp. 269–78). New York: Routledge.

Mahon, E. A. (2006). High-stakes testing and English language learners: Questions of validity. *Bilingual Research Journal, 30* (2), 479–97.

Martinez, M., & Fernández, E. (2004). Latinos at community colleges. *New Directions for Student Services, 2004* (105), 51–62.

Matsuda, M., Lawrence, C., Delgado, R., & Crenshaw, K. (1993). *Words that wound: Critical race theory, assaultive speech, and the first amendment*. Boulder, CO: Westview Press.

McCurdy, J. (1968, March 17). Demands made by east side high school students listed. *Los Angeles Times*, pp. C1, C4–C5.

McNeil, L. M. (2005). Faking equity: High-stakes testing and the education of Latino youth. In A. Valenzuela (Ed.), *Leaving children behind: How "Texas-style" accountability fails Latino youth* (pp. 57–111). Albany: State University of New York Press.

McNeil, L. M., & Valenzuela, A. (2001). The harmful impact of the TAAS system of testing in Texas: Beneath the accountability rhetoric. In G. Orfield & M. L. Kornhaber (Eds.), *Raising standards or raising barriers? Inequality and high-stakes testing in education* (pp. 127–50). New York: Century Foundation Press.

Mehta, S. (2006, June 2). Exit exam leaves 2006 class 42,000 short. *Los Angeles Times*, p. B4.

Menchaca, M. (1995). *The Mexican outsiders: A community history of marginalization and discrimination in California*. Austin: University of Texas Press.

Menchaca, M. (1997). Early racist discourses: The roots of deficit thinking. In R. R. Valencia (Ed.), *The evolution of deficit thinking: Educational thought and practice* (p. 270). London: Falmer Press.

Menchaca, M. (2001). *Recovering history, constructing race: The Indian, black and white roots of Mexican Americans*. Austin: University of Texas Press.

Montejano, D. (1987). *Anglos and Mexicans in the making of Texas, 1836–1986*. Austin: University of Texas Press.

Moore, C., & Shulock, N. (2007). Beyond the open door: Increasing students' success in the California community colleges. Sacramento, CA: Institute for Higher Education Leadership and Policy.

Motel, S., & Patten, E. (2012a). The 10 largest Hispanic origin groups: Characteristics, ranking, top counties. Washington, DC: Pew Hispanic Center.

Motel, S., & Patten, E. (2012b). Hispanics of Mexican origin in the United States, 2010. Washington, DC: Pew Hispanic Center.

Muñoz, L. K. (2001). Separate but equal? A case study of *Romo v. Laird* and Mexican American education. *OAH Magazine of History, 15* (2), 28–35.

National Center for Education Statistics. (2001). *Condition of education 2001* (NCES 2001–072). Washington, DC: U.S. Government Printing Office.

National Center for Education Statistics. (2013). *Digest of education statistics, table 203.50. Enrollment and percentage distribution of enrollment in public elementary and secondary schools, by race/ethnicity and region: Selected years, fall 1995 through fall 2023*. Washington, DC: U.S. Department of Education.

National Center for Education Statistics. (2014). *The nation's report card*. Washington, DC: U.S. Department of Education.

Nieto, S. (2002). *Language, culture and teaching: Critical perspectives for a new century*. Mahwah, NJ: Lawrence Erlbaum.

Nuñez, A.-M., & Crisp, G. (2012). Ethnic diversity and Latino/a college access: A comparison of Mexican American and Puerto Rican beginning college students. *Journal of Diversity in Higher Education, 5* (2), 78–95.

Oakes, J. (1985). *Keeping track: How schools structure inequality*. New Haven, CT: Yale University Press.

Oakes, J. (1990). *Multiplying inequalities: The effects of race, social class, and tracking on opportunities to learn mathematics and science*. Santa Monica, CA: RAND Corporation.

Oakes, J. (1995). Two cities' tracking and within-school segregation. *Teachers College Record, 96* (4), 681–90.

Oakes, J., Gamoran, A., & Page, R. (1992). Curriculum differentiation: Opportunities, outcomes, and meanings. In P. Jackson (Ed.), *Handbook of research on curriculum* (pp. 570–608). New York: MacMillan.

Oakes, J., & Guiton, G. (1995). Matchmaking: The dynamics of high school tracking decisions. *American Educational Research Journal, 32*, 3–33.

Oakes, J., Selvin, M., Karoly, L. A., & Guiton, G. (1992). *Educational matchmaking: Academic and vocational tracking in comprehensive high schools*. Santa Monica, CA: RAND Corporation.

Oakes, J., & Wells, A. S. (1996). *Beyond the technicalities of school reform: Policy lessons from detracking schools*. Los Angeles: UCLA Graduate School of Education and Information Studies.

Ochoa, G. (2004). *Becoming neighbors in a Mexican American community: Power, conflict and solidarity*. Austin: University of Texas Press.

Ochoa, G. (2013). *Academic profiling: Latinos, Asian Americans, and the achievement gap*. Minneapolis: University of Minnesota Press.

Oliverez, P. M. (2006a). *Ready but restricted: An examination of the challenges of college access and financial aid for college-ready undocumented students in the*

U.S. Unpublished doctoral dissertation, University of Southern California, Los Angeles.

Oliverez, P. M. (2006b). Too little, but not too late: A discussion of policies and practices shaping college access for undocumented immigrant students in the United States. *Newsletter of the Association for the Study of Higher Education, 19* (1), 4–7.

Orfield, G. (2001). *Schools more separate: Consequences of a decade of resegregation.* Cambridge, MA: The Civil Rights Project, Harvard University.

Orfield, G., Bachmeier, M. D., James, D. R., & Eitle, T. (1997). Deepening segregation in American public schools: A special report from the Harvard Project on school desegregation. *Equity & Excellence in Education, 30* (2), 5–24.

Orfield, G., Frankenberg, E., Ee, J., & Kuscera, J. (2014). *Brown at 60: Great progress, a long retreat and an uncertain future.* Los Angeles: The Civil Rights Project/Proyecto Derechos Civiles at UCLA.

Orfield, G., & Lee, C. I. (2005). *Why segregation matters: Poverty and educational inequality.* Cambridge, MA: The Civil Rights Project, Harvard University.

Orfield, G., & Lee, C. I. (2006). *Racial transformation and the changing nature of segregation.* Cambridge, MA: The Civil Rights Project, Harvard University.

Orfield, G., & Lee, C. I. (2007). *Historic reversals, accelerating resegregation, and the need for new integration strategies.* Los Angeles: The Civil Rights Project/Proyecto Derechos Civiles at UCLA.

Orfield, G., & Yun, J. T. (1999). *Resegregation in American schools.* Cambridge, MA: The Civil Rights Project, Harvard University.

Ornelas, A. (2002). *An examination of the resources and barriers in the transfer function and process: A case study analysis of an urban community college.* Unpublished doctoral dissertation, University of California, Los Angeles.

Ornelas, A., & Solórzano, D. G. (2004). Transfer conditions of Latina/o community college students: A single institution case study. *Community College Journal of Research and Practice, 28* (3), 233–48.

Ortiz, V. (1996). The Mexican-origin population: Permanent working class or emerging middle class? In V. Ortiz (Ed.), *Ethnic Los Angeles* (pp. 247–77). New York: Russell Sage Foundation.

Ovando, C. J., Combs, M. C., & Collier, V. P. (2006). *Bilingual and ESL classrooms: Teaching in multicultural contexts.* New York: McGraw-Hill.

Park, R. E. (1950). *Race and culture.* Glencoe, IL: Free Press.

Park, R. E., & Burgess, E. W. (1924). *Introduction to the science of sociology.* Chicago: University of Chicago Press.

Perez, E. (1999). *The decolonial imaginary: Writing Chicanas into history.* Bloomington and Indianapolis: Indiana University Press.

Perez Huber, L., Huidor, O., Malagon, M. C., Sanchez, G., & Solórzano, D. G. (2006). *Falling through the cracks: Critical transitions in the Latina/o educational pipeline* (Latina/o Education Summit Report). Los Angeles: UCLA Chicano Studies Research Center.

Perez Huber, L., Malagon, M., & Solórzano, D. G. (2009). *Struggling for opportunity: Undocumented AB540 in the Latina/o pipeline* (CSRC Research Report no. 13). Los Angeles: UCLA Chicano Studies Research Center.

Pew Hispanic Center. (2009). *Between two worlds: How young Latinos come of age in America*. Washington, DC: Pew Hispanic Center.

Pew Hispanic Center and Kaiser Family Foundation. (2004). *The 2004 national survey of Latinos: Education*. Washington, DC: Pew Hispanic Center and Kaiser Family Foundation.

Ramirez, D. J., Yuen, S. D., Ramey, D. R., & Pasta, D. J. (1991). *Final report: Longitudinal study of structured English immersion strategy, early-exit and late-exit transitional bilingual education programs for language-minority children*. San Mateo, CA: Aguirre International.

Rendon, L., Justiz, M., & Resta, P. (1988). *Transfer education in Southwest border community colleges*. Columbia: University of South Carolina.

Rendon, L., & Nora, A. (1997). *Student academic progress: Key trends. Report prepared for the National Center for Urban Partnerships*. New York: Ford Foundation.

Richwine, J. (2009). *IQ and immigration policy*. Unpublished doctoral dissertation, Harvard University, Massachusetts.

Rivas, M. A., Perez, J., Alvarez, C. R., & Solórzano, D. G. (2007). *Latina/o transfer students: Understanding the critical role of the transfer process in California's postsecondary institutions*. Los Angeles: UCLA Chicano Studies Research Center.

Rueda, R., Artiles, A. J., Salazar, J., & Higareda, I. (2002). An analysis of special education as a response to the diminished academic achievement of Chicano/Latino students: An update. In R. R. Valencia (Ed.), *Chicano school failure and success: Past, present, and future* (pp. 310–32). New York: RoutledgeFalmer.

Rumberger, R. (2006). *The growth of the linguistic minority population in the U.S. and California, 1980–2005, EL facts* (Vol. 8). Santa Barbara: UC Linguistic Minority Research Institute.

Rumberger, R., & Rodriguez, G. (2011). Chicano dropouts. In R. R. Valencia (Ed.), *Chicano school failure and success: Past, present, and future* (pp. 76–98). New York: Routledge.

Ryan, C. L., & Siebens, J. (2012). Educational attainment in the United States: 2009 (U.S. Department of Commerce, Trans.). *Current Population Reports*. Washington, DC: U.S. Census Bureau.

Saenz, V. B., & Ponjuan, L. (2008). The vanishing Latino male in higher education. *The Journal of Hispanic Higher Education, 8* (1), 54–89.

San Miguel Jr., G. (1987). *Let all of them take heed: Mexican Americans and the campaign for educational equality in Texas, 1910–1981*. Austin: University of Texas Press.

San Miguel Jr., G. (1988). Culture and education in the American Southwest: Towards an explanation of Chicano school attendance, 1850–1940. *Journal of American Ethnic History, 7* (2), 5–21.

San Miguel Jr., G. (1999). The schooling of Mexicans in the Southwest, 1848–1891. In J. F. Moreno (Ed.), *The elusive quest for equality: 150 years of Chicano/Chicana education* (pp. 31–51). Cambridge, MA: Harvard Educational Review.

San Miguel Jr., G., & Valencia, R. R. (1998). From the Treaty of Guadalupe Hidalgo to Hopwood: The educational plight and struggle of Mexican Americans in the Southwest. *Harvard Educational Review, 68* (3), 353–413.

Sandoval, C. (2000). *Methodology of the oppressed*. Minneapolis: University of Minnesota Press.

Scribner, J. D., & Reyes, P. (1999). Creating learning communities for high-performing Hispanic students: A conceptual framework. In P. Reyes, J. D. Scribner, & A. P. Scribner (Eds.), *Lessons from high-performing Hispanic schools: Creating learning communities* (pp. 188–210). New York: Teachers College Press.

Shockley, J. S. (1974). *Chicano revolt in a Texas town*. South Bend, IN: University of Notre Dame Press.

Snyder, T. D., & Dillow, S. A. (2011). *Digest of education statistics 2010* (NCES 2011-015). Washington, DC: National Center for Education Statistics.

Snyder, T. D., & Dillow, S. A. (2013). *Digest of education statistics 2012* (NCES 2014-015). Washington, DC: National Center for Education Statistics.

Solórzano, D. G. (1993). *The road to the doctorate for California's Chicanas and Chicanos: A study of Ford Foundation minority fellows* (CPS Report). Berkeley: University of California, California Policy Seminar.

Solórzano, D. G. (1998). Critical race theory, race and gender microaggressions, and the experience of Chicana and Chicano scholars. *International Journal of Qualitative Studies in Education, 11* (1), 121–36

Solórzano, D. G., & Delgado Bernal, D. (2001). Examining transformational resistance through a critical race and LatCrit theory framework: Chicana and Chicano students in an urban context. *Urban Education, 36*, 308–42.

Solórzano, D. G., Rivas, M. A., & Velez, V. N. (2005). *Community college as a pathway to Chicana/o doctorate production* (Vol. 11). Los Angeles: UCLA Chicano Studies Research Center.

Solórzano, D. G., & Solórzano, R. W. (1995). The Chicano educational experience: A framework for effective schools in Chicano communities. *Educational Policy, 9*, 293–314.

Solórzano, D. G., & Yosso, T. J. (2000). Toward a critical race theory of Chicana and Chicano education. In C. Martinez, Z. Leonardo, & C. Tejeda (Eds.), *Charting new terrains of Chicana(o)/Latina(o) education* (pp. 35–65). Cresskill, NJ: Hampton Press.

Solórzano, R. W. (2008). High stakes testing: Issues, implications, and remedies for English language learners. *Review of Educational Research, 78* (2), 260–329.

Soto, L. D. (1997). *Language, culture, and power: Bilingual families and the struggle for quality education*. Albany: State University of New York Press.

Spring, J. H. (2011). *The American school: A global context from the Puritans to the Obama era* (8th ed.). New York: McGraw-Hill.

Stanton-Salazar, R. D. (1997). A social capital framework for understanding the socialization of racial minority children and youths. *Harvard Educational Review, 67* (1), 1–40.

Stanton-Salazar, R. D. (2001). *Manufacturing hope and despair: The school and kin support networks of U.S.-Mexican youth*. New York: Teachers College Press.

Stanton-Salazar, R. D., & Dornbusch, S. M. (1995). Social capital and the reproduction of inequality: Information networks among Mexican-origin high school students. *Sociology of Education, 68* (2), 116–35.

Stetser, M., & Stillwell, R. (2014). *Public high school four-year on-time graduation rates and event dropout rates: School years 2010–11 and 2011–12* (NCES 2014–391). Washington, DC: National Center for Education Statistics.

Suarez, A. L. (2003). Forward transfer: Strengthening the educational pipeline for Latino community college students. *Community College Journal of Research and Practice, 27*, 95–117.

Swail, W. S., Cabrera, A. F., & Lee, C. I. (2004). *Latino youth and the pathway to college*. Washington, DC: Pew Hispanic Center.

Talavera-Bustillos, V. (1998). *Chicana college choice and resistance: An exploratory study of first-generation Chicana college students*. Unpublished doctoral dissertation, University of California, Los Angeles.

Talavera-Bustillos, V. (2007). Chicanas and transformational resistance: Analyzing college aspirations within the family context. In J. Figueroa, B. Baker, & B. Mosupyoe (Eds.), *Introduction to ethnic studies* (2nd ed., pp. 453–67). Dubuque, IA: Kendall Hunt.

Taylor, P., Lopez, M. H., Martinez, J., & Velasco, G. (2012). *When labels don't fit: Hispanics and their views of identity*. Washington, DC: Pew Research Center.

Telles, E. E., & Ortiz, V. (2008). *Generations of exclusion: Mexican Americans, assimilation, and race*. New York: Russell Sage Foundation.

Tse, L. (2001). *"Why don't they learn English?" Separating fact from fallacy in the U.S. language debate*. New York: Teachers College Press.

Thomas, W. P., & Collier, V. P. (1997). *School effectiveness for language minority students*. Washington, DC: National Clearinghouse for English Language Acquisition (NCELA).

U.C. Language Minority Research Institute. (2000). Academic English key to academic long term success in school. *Newsletter, 9* (4), 1–2.

Valdés, G. (1996). *Con respeto: Bridging the distances between culturally diverse families and schools: An ethnographic portrait*. New York: Teachers College Press.

Valdés, G., & Figueroa, R. A. (1994). *Bilingualism and testing: A special case of bias*. Norwood, NJ: Ablex.

Valencia, R. R. (Ed.). (1997a). *The evolution of deficit thinking: Educational thought and practice*. London: Falmer Press.

Valencia, R. R. (1997b). Genetic pathology model of deficit thinking. In R. R. Valencia (Ed.), *The evolution of deficit thinking: Educational thought and practice* (pp. 41–112). London: Falmer Press.

Valencia, R. R. (1999). Educational testing and Mexican American students: Problems and prospects. In J. F. Moreno (Ed.), *Elusive quest for equality: 150 years of Chicano/Chicana education* (2nd ed., pp. 123–39). Cambridge, MA: Harvard Educational Review.

Valencia, R. R. (2002a). The plight of Chicano students: An overview of schooling conditions and outcomes. In R. R. Valencia (Ed.), *Chicano school failure and success: Past, present, and future* (pp. 3–51). New York: RoutledgeFalmer.

Valencia, R. R. (Ed.). (2002b). *Chicano school failure and success: Past, present, and future* (2nd ed.). New York: RoutledgeFalmer.

Valencia, R. R. (2008). *Chicano students and the courts: The Mexican American legal struggle for educational equality*. New York: New York University Press.

Valencia, R. R. (Ed.). (2011a). *Chicano school failure and success: Past, present, and future* (3rd ed.). New York: Routledge.

Valencia, R. R. (2011b). Segregation, desegregation, and integration of Chicano students. In R. R. Valencia (Ed.), *Chicano school failure and success: Past, present, and future* (3rd ed., pp. 42–75). New York: Routledge.

Valencia, R. R., & Guadarrama, I. (1996). High-stakes testing and its impact on racial and ethnic minority students. In L. A. Suzuki, P. J. Meller, & J. G. Ponterotto (Eds.), *Handbook of multicultural assessment: Clinical, psychological, and educational applications* (pp. 561–610). San Francisco: Jossey-Bass.

Valencia, R. R., Menchaca, M., & Donato, R. (2002). Segregation, desegregation, and integration of Chicano students: Old and new realities. In R. R. Valencia (Ed.), *Chicano school failure and success: Past, present, and future* (2nd ed., pp. 70–113). New York: RoutledgeFalmer.

Valencia, R. R., & Solórzano, D. G. (1997). Contemporary deficit thinking. In R. R. Valencia (Ed.), *The evolution of deficit thinking: Educational thought and practice* (pp. 160–210). London: Falmer Press.

Valencia, R. R., & Suzuki, L. A. (2001). *Intelligence testing and minority students: Foundations, performance factors, and assessment issues*. Thousand Oaks, CA: Sage.

Valencia, R. R., & Villarreal, B. J. (2011). Gifted Chicano students: Underrepresentation issues and best-case practices for identification and placement. In R. R. Valencia (Ed.), *Chicano school failure and success: Past, present, and future* (3rd ed., pp. 235–54). New York: Routledge.

Valencia, R. R., Villarreal, B. J., & Salinas, M. F. (2002). Educational testing and Chicano students: Issues, consequences and prospects for reform. In R. R. Valencia (Ed.), *Chicano school failure and success: Past, present, and future* (pp. 253–309). New York: RoutledgeFalmer.

Valenzuela, A. (1999). *Subtractive schooling: U.S.-Mexican youth and the politics of caring*. Albany: State University of New York Press.

Valenzuela, A. (2005). Introduction: The accountability debate in Texas: Continuing the conversation. In A. Valenzuela (Ed.), *Leaving children behind: How "Texas-style" accountability fails Latino youth* (pp. 1–32). Albany: State University of New York Press.

Washington Higher Education Coordinating Board. (2010). *2009–2010 tuition and fee rates: A national comparison*. Olympia: Washington Higher Education Coordinating Board.

Wells, A. S., & Oakes, J. (1996). Potential pitfalls of systemic reform: Early lessons from research on detracking. *Sociology of Education, 69*, 135–43.

Willig, A. (1985). A meta-analysis of selected studies on the effectiveness of bilingual education. *Review of Educational Research, 55* (3), 269–317.

Wollenberg, C. (1978). *All deliberate speed: Segregation and exclusion in California schools, 1855–1975*. Berkeley: University of California Press.

Wong Filmore, L. (1991). When learning a second language means losing the first. *Early Childhood Research Quarterly, 6* (3), 232–346.

Yosso, T. J. (2000). *A critical race and LatCrit approach to media literacy: Chicana/o resistance to visual microaggressions*. Unpublished doctoral dissertation, University of California, Los Angeles.

Yosso, T. J. (2005). Whose culture has capital? A critical race theory discussion of community cultural wealth. *Race, Ethnicity, and Education, 8* (1), 69–91.

Yosso, T. J. (2006). *Critical race counterstories along the Chicana/Chicano educational pipeline*. New York: Routledge.

Yosso, T. J., Smith, W., Ceja, M., & Solórzano, D. G. (2009). Critical race theory, racial microaggressions, and campus racial climate for Latina/o undergraduates. *Harvard Educational Review, 79* (4), 659–91.

Yosso, T. J., & Solórzano, D. G. (2006). *Leaks in the Chicana and Chicano educational pipeline* (Latino Policy & Issues Brief). Los Angeles: UCLA Chicano Studies Research Center.

Court Cases

Alvarez v. Lemon Grove School District, Civil Action No. 66625 (Superior Court, San Diego County, CA. 1931).

Aspira of New York, Inc. v. Board of Education of the City of New York, Civil Action No. 72—4002, 394 F. Supp. 1161 (S.D.N.Y. 1975).

Brown v. Board of Education of Topeka, 347 U.S. 483 (1954).

Brown v. Board of Education of Topeka, 349 U.S. 294 (1955).

Castañeda v. Pickard, 648 F. 2d 989 (5th Cir. 1981).

Cisneros v. Corpus Christi Independent School District, 324 F. Supp. 599 (S.D. Tex. 1970).

Delgado v. Bastrop Independent School District, Civil Action No. 388 (W.D. Tex. 1948).

Fisher v. University of Texas at Austin, 133 U.S. 2411 (2013).

GI Forum v. Texas Education Agency, 87 F. Supp. 2d 667 (W.D. Tex. 2000).

Gratz v. Bollinger, 539 U.S. 244 (2003).

Grutter v. Bollinger, 539 U.S. 306 (2003).

Hopwood v. Texas, 78 F.3d 932 (1996).

Independent School District v. Salvatierra, 33 S.W. 2d 790 (Tex. Civ. App., San Antonio 1930).

Keyes v. School District No. 1 Denver, Colorado, 413 U.S. 189 (D. Colo. 1973).

Keyes v. School District No. 1 Denver, 521 F.2d 465 (10th Cir.1975).

Lau v. Nichols, 414 U.S. 563, 94 S. Ct. 786, 39 L. Ed. 2d 1.(1974).

Mendez v. Westminster, 64 F. Supp. 544 (S.D. Cal. 1946).

Milliken v. Bradley, 418 U.S. 717 (1974).

Plessy v. Ferguson, 163 U.S. 537 (1896).

Plyler v. Doe, 457 U.S. 202 (1982).

Regents of the University of California v. Bakke, 438 U.S. 265 (1978).

Romo v. Laird, Civil Action No. 21617 (Superior Court, Maricopa County, AZ. 1925).

INDEX

Page numbers in *italics* represent illustrations.

Equal Protection Clause of U.S. Constitution, 26, 27, 101–2

familial capital, 125, 145, 146; funds of knowledge, 126–27
family: aspirational capital, 124, 145; support of, 110–11
50-50 model, 82–83
first-generation college students, 98
Fisher v. University of Texas at Austin, 103
frameworks, 31–32, 34
Freire, Paulo, 129–30
funds of knowledge, 126–27

gender differences: Chicana feminisms, 121–22; Chicano movement, 121; higher education, 96; microaggressions, 111; stereotypes, 111–13
generational differences: college completion rates, 95–96; language issues, 89–90
genetic deficit thinking, 13–14
gerrymandered district lines, 26
GI Forum v. Texas Education Agency, 56
Gifted and Talented Education (GATE), 53–54; giftedness as socially constructed, 54; language issues, 53; testing for entry to programs, 52–53
graduate degrees, 107–11; factors affecting success, 109–11
Gratz v. Bollinger, 102
Grutter v. Bollinger, 102

hegemony/hegemonic worldview, 117
higher education, 93; anti-affirmative action court cases and legislation, 101–3; Chicana students, 122; college-readiness gap, 97, 146; community college, 103–5; degree completion, 38, *38*; doctoral degrees, 108–9; factors affecting, 96–98; family support, 109; figures comparing enrollments, 93–95; generational and gender differences, 95–96; graduate degrees, 107–11; institutional supports, 106–7; microaggressions, 110–11; race as factor in admissions, 101–3; resilience and resistance, 111–13; transfer to four-year institutions, 104–6, 149; undocumented students, 99–100
high-performing schools, 137–38
high school completion rates, 36, 37, 38, 94–95
high school exit exams, 55–56; English learners, 76–77
high-stakes testing, 55–58; as gatekeeper for educational mobility, 53; defined, 55; "get tough" approach of, 55; negative effects, 55–56; segregation related, 48. *See also* educational testing; No Child Left Behind (NCLB)
Hispanic, use of term, 6
history: Anglo-centric dominant narrative, 120; language use in US, 69–72; Mexican American schooling, 16–31; Mexican history ban, 23, 24; public schools, 11; of segregation, 16–22
home-school partnerships, 132–35
Hopwood v. Texas, 102, 103
human agency, 116, 143–44
hybridity, 121, 147

immigrants/immigration: Americanization programs, 22; fear of, 85; historical Mexican, 69; home-school partnerships, 133–34; importance of learning English, 72–73; intelligence testing related, 15–16; language issue, 69; misunderstandings with school personnel, 133–34; myths about language use, 72–73; special education programs, 54; undocumented students, 27, 99–100; US as nation of immigrants, 69–70; value of education, 4

Independent School District v. Salvatierra, 25

institutional agents, 127–28

intelligence tests, 13–14; alternative forms, 58; immigration policy and, 15–16; recent research, 15–16; scores compared, 21; special education assessment, 52, 54; intelligence, theories of, 67

Isbell School, 18, *19*, 20

Keyes v. School District No. 1, 44–45

knowledge: Chicana feminism on, 122–23; funds of knowledge, 126–27; nature of, 117; normative, 123; traditional teaching models, 128; transformative pedagogies, 128–29

labor market: Americanization programs benefiting employers, 23–24; need for cheap labor, 21–22; social reproduction theories on, 32; stratified, 14, 21–22; training for, 15, 21

language: academic English, 79; as justification for segregation, 21, 26, 27; "assets view," 89; author's skills, 7; Chicano English dialects, 90; contentious battles, 69–72; content of bilingual programs, 82; cultural reproduction theory, 123; diversity in

skills, 5–6; English skills, 5; German in early US, 72; gifted programs, 53, 54; history in US, 69–72; immigrant family interactions, 134–35; importance of learning English, 72–73; improving school practice, 146–47; later-generation Mexican Americans (LGMA), 89–90; limited English proficient (LEP) students, 52; linguistic capital, 124–25; linguistic minority learners, and political climate, 9; oral proficiency in English, 79; policies and politics, 9; prohibitions against speaking Spanish, 23, 72; reasons to maintain native languages, 88–89; so-called language deficits, 15; Spanglish, 146–47

later-generation Mexican Americans (LGMA), 89–90

Latina and Latino critical race theory (LatCrit), 34, 118–21

Latino: college enrollment and completion, 93–95; drop-out rates compared, 39; intensified segregation, 45–46, *45*; overrepresentation in special education programs, 54; population growth, 47; use of term, 6

Latino/White exposure index, 46–47, *46*

Lau v. Nichols, 80–81

lesbian, gay, bisexual and transgender (LGBT), 119

limited English proficient (LEP) students, 52, 86

linguistic capital, 124–25, 146

linguistic minority learners, 73–74; academic English, 79; achievement gap, 74–77; bilingual education issue, 79–82; bilingual education programs, 82–83; English-only

transitional (early exit) bilingual education, 81, 82
Treaty of Guadalupe, 17

undocumented students, 27, 99–100, 143–44

White: college completion rates, 93–94, *94*; Latino/White exposure index, 46–47, *46*; meritocracy, 119–20; Mexican Americans as "other white," 44–45; option to choose their school, 27; students with Mexican American students, 20–21; use of term, 6

xenophobia, 71

Yarborough, Ralph W., 30, *31*

ABOUT THE AUTHOR

Estela Godinez Ballón is a professor in the Liberal Studies Department at California State Polytechnic University, Pomona. She has a PhD in sociology from the University of California, Los Angeles. She also studied at Grossmont Community College and graduated from San Diego State University. Her academic interests include curriculum tracking, Chicana/o education, and women of color in academia.